CONQUER WHAT'S NEXT

*Scheme Your Dream,
Get Your Rear in Gear,
and Gain the Grit to Go **THERE**.*

BILL McCONNELL

I applaud Bill taking action to leave his comfort zone and pursue his THERE. As someone who firmly believes in the power of purpose, I appreciate how Bill begins the process of Conquering What's Next by focusing on the question 'Why am I here?' I hope you find inspiration from Bill's journey to take the next step on yours.

Kevin Monroe, Host of the
Higher Purpose Podcast

If you want to get my attention with your book you need to challenge me, inspire me, and (most important) make me think. Then you need to deliver something I can use, and back it up with experiences and examples that make it real. That's exactly what Bill McConnell does in Conquer What's Next. Read it, grab the advice that resonates, and make the choice to go THERE!

Michael Hudson, Host of the
Get Your Message Heard Podcast

The world is filled with underdeveloped wishes, would-be expeditions, and lifelong dreams that carry the label "someday." Bill McConnell is one of the exceptions. His book gives us hope and shows us how to conquer our dreams once and for all.

Kary Oberbrunner, author of
Elixir Project and Day Job to Dream Job

"After reading Bill's second writing achievement, the words "Been There, Done That" take on a whole new meaning. Bill has an amazing ability to combine his brand of humor, stories, sound principles, insight from experts and personal experiences to weave together a practical and insightful approach to getting you THERE, wherever your THERE may be! Thank you, Bill, for making it easy to understand and providing simple examples to follow. My THERE is definitely within reach!"

Jamey French, speaker, trainer & coach

"After watching Bill apply these principles to his own pursuit of mountains and other goals and having used elements of the plan in my own life, I can testify that this method works! His program will definitely get you There!"

Timothy R. Johnston, P.E., President,
Vallevue Consulting, LLC

CONQUER WHAT'S NEXT

AUTHOR ACADEMY elite

Also by this Author
Together
The Best Marriage Advice You'll Ever Get
When It Comes to Your Career

Copyright© 2018 Bill McConnell
All rights reserved.

Printed in the United States of America

Published by Author Academy Elite
P.O. Box 43 Powell OH 43035

www.AuthorAcademyElite.com

All Scripture quotations, unless otherwise indicated, are taken from the Holy Bible, New International Version®, NIV®. Copyright ©1973, 1978, 1984, 2011 by Biblica, Inc.™ Used by permission of Zondervan. All rights reserved worldwide. www.zondervan.com The "NIV" and "New International Version" are trademarks registered in the United States Patent and Trademark Office by Biblica, Inc.™

All rights reserved. No part of this publication may be reproduced, stored in a retrieval system, or transmitted in any form or by any means—for example, electronic, photocopy, recording—without the prior written permission of the publisher. The only exception is brief quotations in printed reviews.

Paperback ISBN-13: 978-1-64085-195-5

Hardcover ISBN-13: 978-1-64085-196-2

Library of Congress Number: 2018900461

DEDICATION

No one succeeds alone. No one achieves alone.
This book is dedicated to my wife, Lisa,
and my daughter, Shelby.
Both are models of conquering
whatever comes next in their lives.
Together, they are my reasons for conquering
whatever comes next in mine.

CONTENTS

Introduction
xv

1. I Want to Go There
1

2. The Construct of Repeated Achievement
11

PART 1 – SCHEME YOUR DREAM

3. The Bigger Picture of Purpose
23

4. The Gift of Goal Setting
45

5. The Measure of Identified Motives
61

PART 2 – GET YOUR REAR IN GEAR

6. The Hub of Daily Motives
83

7. The Revealing of Routines
101

8. The Admission of Needed Adjustment
109

PART 3 – GAIN THE GRIT TO GO FOR IT

9. The Resilience of Resolve
127

10. The Stockpile of Support
145

11. The Reward of Repetition
155

PART 4 – FLOW

12. Why Habits Are the Hub of Achievement
165

13. How Your Day Affects Your Life
175

14. The AchievementOptimizer™ Visualized
187

15. There You Go Again
193

Acknowledgments
197

Endnotes
199

About the Author
203

*The internet tells thousands of stories
of individuals who've reached
for the improbable and
achieved the impossible.*

*And there are millions upon millions
of people who view those stories
and wish it were them.*

*Many choose to stay Here.
Few choose to go **There**.*

*I want you to become the few.
I want you to go **There**,
and I'm going to show you how.*

INTRODUCTION

There . . . bold and capitalized.

Every time you see the word **There** and the T is capitalized, it is significant.
It is referring to your **There**.
Not my **There**.
Not my daughter's **There**.
Your **There**. Your goal.
Your purpose lived out in an event, adventure, career, trek, weekend, semester, season, life direction, game, dream, passion, you-name-it.
It's your **There** and no one else's.
I want you to get **There**.
There is where you want to be, not where you currently are.
My **There**, as you will read in the chapters ahead, has been volcanos, mountains, getting off a dock without getting wet, youth camps, mission trips, writing this book, and so on.
The way to get **There** will fit into your life no matter what your life looks like right now.
There is possible and here are the steps and processes to ensure your success.
Why stay Here when you know your **There** is waiting for you?
So, let's get at it.
Yeah, I went **There**.

1
I WANT TO GO *THERE*

I never thought I would go **There**. Not me. I mean, why would I, right? I'm not meant for that. Not that or the other thing that went with it. Never in my wildest dreams did I ever think of going **There**.

But my daughter went **There**. Because she went there, she inspired me to go **There** as well.

What got me started in this endeavor was a Central American natural catastrophe, better known as an erupting volcano. If you want something to get your attention, an erupting volcano will do it. It happens down in Guatemala more than you think. This one demanded my attention because of my daughter.

My daughter, Shelby, lived in Guatemala as a missionary teaching ESL in a school. She loved it there. Well, a few days before the weekend, she informs us that she and her friend Christoph were going to hike to the top of a volcano. It was an overnight group expedition. Hike up, spend the night near the summit, get up early the next morning so you can experience the sunrise from the top. Cool. What a great hike! No big deal. Lots of folks do this every year.

The evening of the hike, her roommate, Julisa, contacted us by Facebook Messenger. She couldn't reach Shelby by cell and was worried. Ash was falling in Antigua, a town close to the volcano, more than had happened in ten years. Vulcán Fuego was erupting. Julisa wanted to know if we'd heard anything from Shelby. She had no idea whether she was in danger or not. No news was not a good sign.

What did we do back in Colorado? What could we do? Pray. Get others to pray. Pray with others. Keep calling her cell phone. Send her messages. Continue. That's what we did.

We didn't hear from her for several hours. Think about it. If Julisa, who lives there, can't get her on the phone, why would we think we could? Nevertheless, we had to do something. That's what we did. That plus freaking out over the idea that our only daughter would die under a hot lava flow and we'd never see her again.

On top of that, even though she had told us, we didn't remember the name of the volcano she was climbing. Who knew where she was or what mortal danger she was encountering? (We weren't even sure if she had the One Ring with her. You know, in order to drop it off. Save Middle Earth. That sort of thing.) We continued freaking out because that seemed to be our only option and it gave us an outlet for our uncontainable dread.

Several hours later, late into the night, we got a text from her. Are you ready for this one?

"I'm OK. Just sitting here watching a volcano erupt."

She wasn't on Volcán Fuego! She was on Volcán Acatenango, the next one over. A little bit higher and completely dormant. Made sense now. The wind wasn't blowing their way so no ash would bury them. As a result, she had a once-in-a-lifetime opportunity to witness a violently erupting volcano at night from eye-level, while being completely safe. The pictures were amazing. Beats anything you'd find on National Geographic or Netflix for that matter. Now we could chill.

Within the next week, our daughter safely back at work, a personal challenge gripped my aging spirit of adventure. I wanted to climb that volcano. No one could talk me out of it. Not even my wife, who eventually agreed to join me on this trek. Would it be too much to ask for another epic eruption (on Vulcán Fuego, of course) while we were up there? In any case, I set my sights on making that climb.

It's important to note that this climb is a weekend endeavor that people much younger than I decide to do on 24-hours' notice and then go. Kind of like what Shelby and Christoph did. I knew, however, that I needed a little more preparation. Which would require advanced planning.

A year earlier, both my wife and I set a goal to shed the poundage and get in shape. My wife registered to run her first 5K. I was determined to help her. In the process, she lost over 50 pounds, and I shed around 35. This was a good thing. Now I was set on an 8K hike that was 95% up. It's a volcano. What would you expect?

My goal was simple. Climb Volcán Acatenango in June of 2015. I had five months to get ready and a Fitbit. 10,000 steps a day. No compromise. Eat better. Say no to anything that wasn't going to help me reach my goal. Soft drinks? Gone. Chocolate? See ya. Walk the dog. I walked the dog a lot. My dog loved that (she's an Aussie!).

I had this mental image. One of my daughter's fellow trekkers was a professional photographer who captured this hiking group, on the summit of Acatenango, silhouetted against the massive explosion on Volcán Fuego. I wanted to stand **There**. I knew the view probably wouldn't be as spectacular as that photo. Nevertheless, I wanted to be **There**. But I knew that if I didn't plan, pay the guide Q600 ($80 American) in advance, and spend serious time preparing for the climb; such a hike would never happen. Therefore, I committed.

I committed.

Five months out, I was already 100% in. Knowing this got me out of the house every day to walk. Knowing this got me to say no to a lot of food that I love to eat. Knowing this got me to drop by my doctor's office once a week to weigh myself on his scale. I wanted to see progress, but I didn't want to buy my own scale.

My daughter, Shelby, and my wife, Lisa, initially signed on to do this with me. My wife walked more and also adjusted her diet. It was going to be a family affair, a McConnell outing for the ages.

I want you to understand my daughter a little bit. She's a joiner. Not just anything. She's a smart joiner. She finds out what she's getting into beforehand, makes an informed decision, and jumps in. She played soccer in middle school and was pretty good at it. She never scored a single goal. When she did score, it was always at least two goals in the game. She did that more than once. Dad was proud. Still is.

Since soccer was not foreign to her and because she loves competing against guys and sweep tackling a lot, she joined a co-ed pick-up weekly soccer game in St Luis, a town close to where she lived in Guatemala. During a game in May 2015 she fell and came down hard on her back. Real hard. Too hard. She couldn't move. There was no ER close and no EMTs nearby, so they picked her up and got her off the hard dirt field where they played.

When we heard about it the next day, there was nothing we could do. We're 2,500 miles away. Any damage was already done. So, my wife, the Family Nurse Practitioner, the family health care provider, jumped into action. She already had given her meds for various possible situations. Those came into play immediately. (Lisa plans ahead for stuff you never want to happen.)

The good news was that nothing was broken, but Shelby had a very, very sore back. The bad news was she wasn't climbing Acatenango in a month. Since she had already been **There**, and had the best view in the world of an erupting volcano to the south—been there, done that—she said, "You go on ahead."

Now my wife, who was joining the trek because Shelby and I were going, decided to back out as well. She and Shelby would do some shopping in the paca instead. (The paca is a used clothing market behind the tourist market. Basically, bargain shopping—and my wife loves bargain shopping.) Both of my ladies are very good at shopping. No challenge for either one of them there. I was alone.

That's okay because I committed to doing this. I cannot make any commitments for anyone else. Neither can you.

I became the lone family volcano climber that year. No longer with the familiar company, I showed up for the evening orientation. Hard for me to do, because I am an almost off-the-scale introvert. Now I was with a group of total strangers from several different countries. Nothing about them was familiar to me. I was all alone in this crowd.

As we gathered at the hostel to get the required info for the weekend ahead, I noticed something. There were twenty-seven people, including two guides, going on this trek. I was the oldest. I later discovered I was the oldest by twenty-five years. Grey hair began to grow a little faster—from my ears. My cue-ball baldness showed no sign of growth.

It was at that point I decided something else. On this trek, I would not be the last one up the hill. Consider it a secondary goal, a silent extra push for me to keep going determinedly. I didn't want to struggle to my destination. I didn't want to hold up the rest of the group. I may have been the oldest, but I wasn't going to be last.

This climb did not require special gear. But I still had forty pounds of stuff on my back. Plus, each person carried part of the group load—supper, breakfast, water, tent, sleeping bag. You know, stuff.

Stuff is okay if you need it. We needed the gear, so I hauled it like everybody else. Well, almost like everybody else. A few people opted to have a donkey carry their load. It was an option. I opted to carry my own.

This hike, obviously, was all uphill on slippery, loose ground. It was volcanic ash that was hiked daily for many years. Ash doesn't pack down very well. It was not very substantial, nor was it fun to hike. You climbed up three feet and slid back half the distance.

At our second rest area, something dawned on me. It was a huge lightbulb that lit up the sky all around me. It blinded me with insight yet did not affect those around me. The lightbulb? I didn't need to haul my own pack or the stuff in the pack. Genius.

How did I come to this conclusion? My original commitment. My goal was to climb this volcano. It did not include hauling forty pounds on my back. It had nothing to do with fitting in with the rest of the crew. It did not involve proving my manliness and maturity. It was not dependent on a team. None of that mattered. My commitment was not based on those things.

I hailed one of the team leaders and ceded my pack to him. He strapped it onto the donkey while I paid 200Q for the option to hike without a pack. It didn't matter what anyone else thought. I wasn't there for them. I was there for me. I was there to reach a goal. The goal did not include heavy weights on my back. Weight eliminated. Adjustment made. On we went.

We stopped for the night at the regular spot. We rose around 3:00 a.m. to climb the final hour to the peak. Crater, more like it, as it is a volcano. We were there as a group for sunrise.

Mission accomplished. Goal realized. I was not the last person to reach the camp, nor was I the last person to reach the top. I realized my five-month goal on schedule. My daily habits and routines got me in shape and up the hill. When I got tired, my reasons and motives kept me going. I made adjustments to keep me on task both before and during the hike.

That was my **There**, not your **There**.

Where, or what, is your **There**?

It could be a volcano. Why not, right? It could be something much more intense, like a Master's degree or living in a certain part of the world. Maybe it's to make a certain amount of money or work for a particular company.

Perhaps it is to walk again after an accident or speak again after a stroke. Maybe it is about getting up in front of a bunch of people and giving a speech, or running a marathon, or starting a business?

You see, it doesn't matter what your **There** is. It's your **There** and no one else's. Not your spouses'. Not your parents. Not your peers. Not your boss'.

Imagine telling your boss where his/her **There** is. You lay it out for the boss. Umm . . . Nope. That won't happen. You know why.

Same for your spouse. Yes, I know you and your spouse are one. You're married to each other. If I'd told my wife her **There** was to be a school teacher instead of a nurse practitioner, she wouldn't have been happy with me then and she wouldn't be happy with me now. Her heart isn't in teaching. It's about caring, caregiving, helping, healing, and mentoring.

You define your own **There**. Whether it's a short-term **There**, like climbing a volcano, or a career **There**, like nursing, engineering, or running your own company. It's your **There**.

I know what you're thinking. You're thinking, "I'm Here. I'm not **There**. And I don't see any way to get **There** from here. Now what?"

That's what we're going to explore. I believe you can get almost anywhere from Here.

Here is not the finish line. Here is the starting line. If Here is where you are at age 61, or age 16, it doesn't matter.

You start Here. Where else are you going to start? You only have two options at this point: start from Here or don't start from Here. I suggest you go with the first option.

The second one is a terrible option. Not starting from Here means going Nowhere. Nowhere should never be an option. When Nowhere is the option you choose, nothing is the result. Nobody wants Nothing. Everybody wants Something, but you can't get Something from Nothing. It's the whole "blood from a turnip" idea. It's not going to happen.

I guess there is a third option. Wait Here for someone else to take you **There**. This option is basically getting someone else to abandon their own **There** for your **There**. This is theft. This is repression, not to mention selfish. Let's not dwell on this option anymore.

Take the first option. Start.

You can get **There** from Here. No one can tell you otherwise. Well, they can tell you anything, you don't have to listen to them. Those going Nowhere have lots of time to tell others they can't go Anywhere either. Tune them out. "Lalalalalala . . . I can't hear you." Good job.

"No matter where you are, there you are."

Somebody who might be famous said that. Look it up. It is a statement that challenges you to "Bloom where you're planted," or "Make the most of your current situation." I'm changing it right now. Maybe my statement will become famous. Why not?

"No matter where you are, Here you are."

Feel free to quote me to your friends on Facebook. Realize that you are Here. Here is not bad, nor is it wrong.

You're simply Here. But you'll never get **There** if you stay Here.

Better yet, commit. Then **"no matter where you are, There you will be."**

I challenge you to find a **There** in your life and start Here. Then do everything in your power to get **There**.

2

THE CONSTRUCT OF REPEATABLE EFFORT

CORE

> *You will never change your life until you change something you do daily. The secret of your success is found in your daily routine.*
> John Maxwell

Nolan Ryan Gets On a Stationary Bike

Thursday morning at 7:30, only 4 1/2 hours after getting to bed, you would have found Nolan Ryan lifting weights in a room underneath Arlington Stadium.

He could have used an extra hour or two of sleep. He could have watched the morning television shows. He could have even answered a few congratulatory phone calls, but he didn't. That would all have to wait.

This was the morning after his seventh no-hitter, recorded on May 1, 1991. This morning, like every other morning, everything else had to wait because Nolan Ryan had work to do.

"My life revolves around my workout routine right now," the Texas Rangers right-hander said at a news conference later in the day. That was about as good an explanation as any for how, at 44-years of age, he had held the Toronto Blue Jays hitless the previous night.[1]

In his 25-year major league career, this was perhaps his most dominating performance. Ryan struck out sixteen and walked only two in a 3-0 victory over the Toronto Blue Jays, the team leading the American League in both hits and runs scored.

Wrap your head around this little-known statistic for some perspective. When pitching for the Angels in 1973, Ryan struck out seventeen and walked four against Detroit—generally regarded as his finest no-hitter. The Angels' second baseman in that game was Sandy Alomar. Sandy's son, Blue Jay second baseman Roberto Alomar, struck out to end Wednesday's game.

Mind. Blown.

This was supposed to be a season of relative tranquility for Ryan, who, amid much fanfare, recorded his 5,000th strikeout in 1989 and earned his 300th victory in 1990. Also, in the 1990 season, on a June night in Oakland, he pitched his sixth no-hitter—and first since 1981—making him the oldest pitcher in major league history to throw a no-hitter.

Later that Thursday, there he was on a platform in a hotel ballroom, taking time out from a day-off appearance at a charitable function to answer questions.

> "I never think about things like that," he said. "Keeping up my career is an ongoing deal, and I have to concern myself with my next game. So, I don't sit around and reflect on what's happening. Once a game's over... Well, it's like this morning. I was down in the weight room preparing myself for my next start. That's what I have to concern myself with—my routine—so I'll be ready.
>
> "That's not to say I didn't hope to be in position to throw another no-hitter and be able to do it in Arlington

for the (Ranger) fans. I'm appreciative it worked out. It was a neat night."[2]

During the season, on the nights he pitched, Ryan rode a stationary bicycle for at least forty-five minutes after the game. Between starts, he spent more than two hours every day lifting weights, running, and biking. Rangers pitching coach, Tom House, said of Ryan, "He's still throwing hard because he does what it takes to prepare himself. He's like the mailman. Nothing keeps him from making his rounds in the weight room."

There it is. Daily habits. Routine. Consistency. That's why Nolan Ryan came to be known as Major League Baseball's Iron-Man. He set himself up as a man of ***conscious, daily activity that he chose to do.*** Focused habits present the best opportunity for achieving success in any field. Deliberate habits helped make Nolan Ryan the greatest major league pitcher of all time. Deliberate habits in your life can help you achieve what you once thought impossible.

Effort Revolving Around One Thing

We are creatures of habit, deliberate or otherwise. We find easy and seemingly functional ways of doing things and repeat the process regularly. Not all these ways are good for us and not all these ways are truly functional. These are habits.

You will get more familiar with this unique definition in the chapter on habits. For now, let it sink in a bit, especially that last part about choosing not to live without it. That habit that gets you closer to your goal. That routine that pushes you forward. That habit that makes you uncomfortable every day, and yet, you do it every single day.

> **Habits are a conscious, daily activity you've chosen not to live without.**

This is the **Construct** (you are building into your life) of **Repeatable** (you did it today and you can do it again tomorrow) **Effort** (you are exerting energy you have toward some objective).

Let's break it down some more.

CORE – The Construct of Repeatable Effort

There are three aspects that must be realized before your achievement is realized.

CONSTRUCT: Habits that you choose to do daily.

The verb is to build or erect. The noun is a theory containing various conceptual elements. Daily habits are both. You're building a better you, on purpose. Consider the theory of achievement through deliberate daily habits.

Charles Duhigg is recognized as an expert when it comes to the idea of habits. He's a reporter for *The New York Times*. He's also *The New York Times* best-selling author of *The Power of Habit*, about the science of habit formation, as well as *Smarter Faster Better: The Secrets of Productivity in Life and Business*.

In *The Power of Habit*, Duhigg breaks down a habit into three primary components.

- Cue: The trigger that sets you up to do a habit.
- Routine: The actual, deliberate habit you want to perform on a regular basis.
- Reward: A positive result of doing the routine. Find a way to become positively addicted to that reward.

Here's a YouTube video link that will help explain it further.

https://www.youtube.com/watch?v=voX0gUn_JOI

The Construct Of Repeatable Effort

Duhigg also explores the following ideas in depth:

- **Keystone Habits:** Identify primary habits in your life that strengthen your other habits. These are the things that build your life and define who you are.
- **Exercise:** Research tells us that exercise is a huge catalyst and a keystone habit for all of us.
- **Willpower:** Willpower ultimately is the engine that drives the whole show. Willpower is essential for building new habits. Probably for this reason, it has been proven that willpower outperforms IQ by a factor of 2 in academic performance.
- **Malleability:** Duhigg tells us that all habits are malleable. Anything that you may have in your life that you're not particularly proud of can be changed. Any habit can be broken. Any habit can be developed. The first step to that is believing that you can.[3]

REPEATABLE: One Action Done Over and Over Again

I love the movie *The Karate Kid*. The original one, in case you're wondering. Cheesy as it may be now, it was great when it first came out. Daniel gets the girl, gains a new best friend and father figure, gets beat up a lot, and eventually comes out the winner. (Sorry, did I spoil it for you? Hope not.)

In an early scene, Daniel wants to learn karate, so he doesn't get beat up all the time. Mr. Miyagi reluctantly agrees to teach him.

Miyagi: "Daniel-san, must talk. Walk on road. Walk right side, safe. Walk left side, safe. Walk middle, sooner or later, get squished, just like grape. Here, karate same thing. Either you karate do 'yes,' or karate do 'no.' You karate do 'guess so,' squish, just like grape. Understand?"

Daniel: "Yeah, I understand."
Miyagi: "Now ready?"
Daniel: "Yeah, I'm ready."
Miyagi: "First make sacred pact. I promise teach karate. That my part. You promise learn. I say, you do. No question. That your part. Deal?
Daniel: "Deal."[4]

Daniel's training begins with washing and waxing five or six cars, repeating a single motion over and over again. Not his idea of intense martial arts training. Nevertheless, he agrees to do whatever Mr. Miyagi asks of him. Wax the cars. Sand a floor. Paint a fence (both sides). Finally, paint a house. (Don't forget to breathe.) Eventually, Daniel breaks down, accusing Mr. Miyagi of making him a slave—free labor with no noticeable return.

The agreement goes both ways. Daniel agrees to do whatever Mr. Miyagi asks. Mr. Miyagi agrees to teach Daniel karate. Without knowing it, by following the how-to instructions of each laborious task, repeating a motion over and over, he unconsciously learns karate. Finally, he loses his temper and confronts Mr. Miyagi with his slave labor idea conclusion.

Mr. Miyagi shows Daniel that his actions, repeated over and over, translated into basic defensive techniques. Blocking punches and kicks will keep Daniel from getting repeatedly bruised and beaten.

Daniel's eyes are opened to what he's learned. He's learned karate. Suddenly, waxing the cars and sanding the floor wasn't labor but training. Painting fences and houses is no longer seen as work, but learning a skill. Wax on, wax off became a way to achieve his goal, and to build character.

Mr. Miyagi looks him in the eyes and says encouragingly, "Come back tomorrow."

Repetition over time creates a habit. There's a lot more

to it than this, but in its simplest form, this statement stands true. Think Charles Duhigg.

Accidental Repetition

When you don't think about some repeatable task you have before you on a daily basis, you do it pretty much the same way every time.

Our brain does it's very best to make us efficient. It does that by doing tasks you don't have to think about. Let's go a little deeper.

Think of tying your shoes. In reality, you don't think about it anymore. Because you learned that skill long ago, now you do it quickly and efficiently the same way every time. Thank your brain for the effortless task. It wasn't effortless, though, when you tried to learn it as a child.

Let's recreate that idea.

What if there was a better way to tie your shoes? Okay, maybe not better, but different. Let's say you have determined to tie your shoes differently for the next three weeks. Look up "tying shoelaces" on YouTube. Find one that's different from how you currently tie yours. Here's an example:

> I'll Never Tie My Shoes the Same Way Again
> https://www.youtube.com/watch?v=bhrf201K90w

Day one: you thought about it. Same with day two. If you stuck with it, eventually it became easier and easier. By the third week, you did it without thinking at all.

I know there are some "habit gurus" who postulate that doing something every day for three weeks makes it a new habit. (By the way, this is not true.) I'm not one of those guys. This happens to be a deliberately new way to do a simple task. Chances are, at some point during those three weeks, you got in a bit of a hurry and tied your shoes the old-fashioned way, without thinking about it. But when you weren't in a rush and you thought about this exercise, you tied your shoes the new way. Well, new to you, at least.

By doing this exercise, you accomplished two things. First, you learned a new way to tie shoes. Congratulations. Second, you turned an accidental habit into a deliberate one.

Deliberate Repetition

Exercise is the best example to run with here. Hehe, run with. Get it? Nobody accidently exercises on a regular basis. "Oops! I accidently ran a 5K again today. My bad." Doesn't happen. Exercise is a habit. It is the deliberate repetition of activity done daily.

As stated earlier, I've defined habits as **a conscious, daily activity you've chosen not to live without.** Habits are created through deliberate repetition.

You will also learn in Chapter 4 that there are two kinds of achievement: Lifestyle Achievements and End-Game Achievements. Lifestyle Achievements require deliberate repetition to create a habit needed to facilitate reaching a life-long goal, such as a certain body weight. End-Game Achievements require creation of habits necessary to get from Here to **There** (the top of a volcano). Michael Hyatt, former CEO of Thomas Nelson Publishing and founding CEO of Michael Hyatt and Company, refers to these as a habit goal or an achievement goal.

EFFORT: Your Hard Work

Can a personal achievement be called an achievement if no hard work is involved? "I got out of bed this morning. What a great achievement!" Hmmm . . . maybe for someone recovering from a significant accident or major surgery. Perhaps even for someone suffering from severe depression. For them, this is hard work. However, speaking personally, I am not in any of those categories. It is not hard work at all for me to get out of bed. No effort at all. Repeatable, yes. Hard work, nope.

Let me tell you at this point that I get up at 4:30 a.m. four days a week. The other three days, I get up at 5:30 a.m. When I first started this, it was extremely hard work. Now that I've done it for over a year, not so much. Having a set bedtime is huge though.

I have to be honest with you though. It is hard work for me to exercise every day. I don't like to do it. Call me lazy if you want, but it won't stick. Why? Because even though I don't like to exercise, I do it every day. It is a deliberate effort.

This exercise goal has two outcomes in its crosshairs: both lifestyle and end-game. I want to weigh 162 pounds by December 1, 133 days from now. I currently weigh 175 pounds in case you're wondering. Getting **There** is one of my optimized end-game target achievements.

I also would like to stay **There**. At least within two pounds either side of **There**. Now it's become a lifestyle achievement. The end-game will get me to the starting point of a new lifestyle.

Eventual Autopilot

Continuing with our exercise example, even though you may not like it, you have to make it a daily activity, rain or shine. It needs to eventually be set on autopilot.

The idea of autopilot in an airplane is amazing. Get in the air with the destination coordinates pre-programmed and push the autopilot button. (In my mind, that's how it works.) Amazing. The computers begin calculating, recalculating, again and again, to adjust for wind, altitude, other planes, and so on. The pilot could take a nap if he wished.

There is no autopilot button to get you **There**. Sorry about that. The closest thing you have to an autopilot is resolve. We'll go deep with resolve in a later chapter. Resolve is what you need to start the habits that will eventually get you **There**. Think of resolve as the autopilot button, except you have to hold it down for a while.

Jimmy Chin is an extreme sports photographer. He went from living in his van to combining two things he loves to do. His label (extreme sports photographer) tells you exactly what he does. He seems to do it better than anyone else.

> *The two great risks are risking too much but also risking too little. That's for each person to decide. For me, not risking anything is worse than death. By far.*
>
> Jimmy Chin

The Construct of Repeatable Effort is your daily decision to take big risks to achieve great things in your life. Those tasks you choose to do daily form the hub of your success.

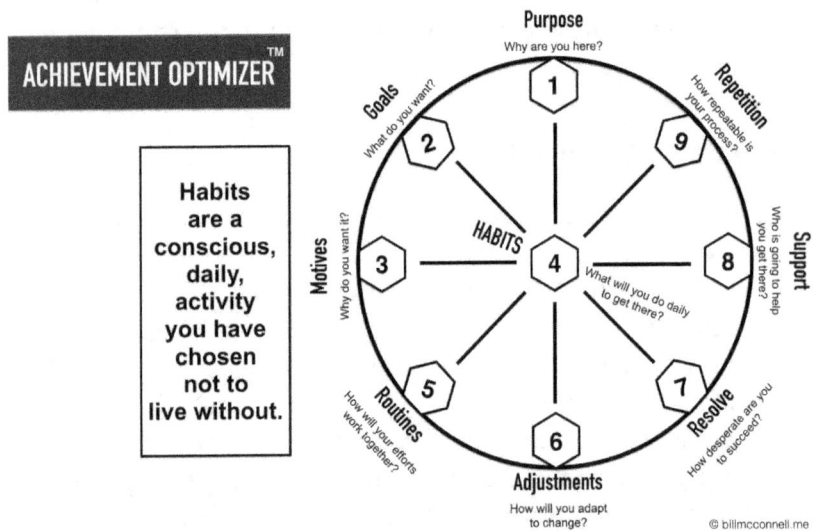

PART I: Scheme Your Dream

*Productivity is never an accident.
It is always the result of a commitment to excellence,
intelligent planning and focused effort.*
Paul J. Meyer

*Planning is bringing the future into the present so that
you can do something about it now.*
Alan Lakein

This is the pen and paper portion of the approach to achieving great things in your life.

Begin to scheme. Secretly and systematically plot your world domination by going after that dream you've chosen to become a reality.

Getting there on paper only means you've made a blueprint. But a blueprint in the hands of a builder is a step in the right direction.

Developing the first three skills and answering the questions will give you an unmistakable blueprint for achieving something unforgettable.

3

THE BIGGER PICTURE OF PURPOSE

Why are you here?

To forget one's purpose is the commonest form of stupidity.
Ruth Benedict

I held strongly to a defining purpose for many years. It was a driving force in my life. It kept me going when life was grand and pushed me forward when things sucked. It was noble. It was spiritual. It was also slowly killing me.

I fell into the trap that my career and calling were forever connected to my purpose in life. Early on I never dreamed that my career path would change. I'm very stubborn in this regard. But what do you do when your career is slowly killing you?

While discussing my future career options with my wife, I discovered I had to let go of what I thought was my purpose. I didn't want to do that. Finally, she said the simplest thing to me, "Do something else."

I was under so much stress from my current situation, I never realized the weight it held over me. In desperate need of relief, I conceded to the idea of a career change. At the very moment that I told my wife, "I'll do something else," I felt a ton or two immediately leave the room. It left my mind, lifted off my shoulders, and freed me from stress, guilt, and perceived failure. It also sent me into an area of life I'd never been before.

I didn't see it initially, but it was there. I was lost. I had inadvertently kissed my purpose goodbye. I traded my life's direction for a lighter load. I was free from the stress and demand of a career I loved. I was released from a job that was sucking the life out of me. Now what?

Skipping ahead several years, I found myself with the same feelings and weights, but with no job to which I could attribute them. It all came to a head one morning after my wife headed off to work. She had a job and I didn't; I felt worthless, useless, a complete failure and burden to my family. I wanted it all to be over.

Within minutes of her leaving I found myself curled up in a fetal position in the corner of the living room. I cried for more than half an hour. Pools of tears needed to be mopped up. I am not exaggerating. I wanted to die. The burden of not knowing a sense of purpose is far greater than the stress of any job or career.

I don't remember what I did the rest of that day. I do know I got through it somehow. Somewhere in there, God spoke softly to me and told me to keep going. I didn't consider it great advice at the time. Something a little more concrete would have helped. Nonetheless, I knew it was God not giving up on me, and I was not about to give up on Him or my family.

My purpose at that time became simple: Just keep going. So that's what I did. My purpose became "One More Day."

Skip ahead a few years. I'm still searching, never giving up, and living one more day. Apparently, I'm a slow learner. It's not the first time I've heard that. The point is I am learning, slowly or otherwise.

The Bigger Picture of Purpose

Funny how a sermon comes along at exactly the right time. I have no clue what our pastor said that evening, but it did compel me to write him an email explaining my situation. Here's what I wrote:

Lisa and I were at the Saturday evening service as this is sometimes our only time to worship together. Your sermon prompted the following thoughts.

God has been silent to me for many years now. In spite of much prayer by myself and others, I have been jobless for almost five years now. My previous jobs were neither wanted nor did they last. Corporate and government cutbacks eliminated both. I am plagued by wasted time and wandering thoughts on more days than can be counted. My attempts to fill my time with worth and purpose have only been met with frustration and dead ends. The more I reach out for help, the less understood I seem to become to those around me.

My wife works 70+ hours a week, and there's nothing I can do to help her cut back and ease our financial strain. Someone even commented that I had it made, with a wife that works so I don't have to. No one realizes the silent hell I'm struggling with. Satan has, on more than one occasion, planted the idea of suicide in my mind. There have been times when my wife would go to work at six in the morning and all I could do was cry for hours after she left.

This year began with me setting 12 goals to strive for. They are very specific and time sensitive. This list has become my daily prayer ever since. Many days, I just fail. Deadlines have already come and gone. My efforts seem useless and yet I keep on working. They are slowly becoming a megaphone of God's silence in my life. I cannot decide what I'm more afraid of at this point—continued failure or of eventual success. The first one I am used to. The second, I'm yet to experience.

Only two goals have been realized thus far: prayer and journaling. The more I pray, it seems the more silent God becomes. The more I journal, the more I see in print the wasted time/effort/money I've recorded.

I could go on writing like this for days, but I think the picture is clear.

And yet, God is more real to me today than He has ever been. I see Amy at Zoë's, closing her eyes and clutching her heart as she sings words that you can see she believes with all her heart. I see Dave Powell raise his arms, and cry out words of adoration in worship, how God is gripping his heart. I watch my wife open her Bible, and take notes during sermons because she doesn't want to miss a single seed of truth that could affect her life or others at some point in the future. I'm reminded of how my daughter lets herself go so freely as she worships God. Her trust in Him alone is so evident. I hear from Shelby how God is using her and others in the school in Tizate, Guatemala, when we Skype every week. She tells us of her hunger to be more involved in intercession and prayer for the mission work there. We pray together, trust together, believe together. When our friend died tragically two years ago, I couldn't imagine how the family could handle it. Yet I saw, still see, God at work in their lives, using the tragedy to draw others to Him.

I read countless stories of how God has answered, and is answering, the prayers of His people. Prayers that are so far beyond anything I could ever dream up or imagine. Prayers that are so trivial I wonder why God even bothers, and yet, He does. Prayers so impossible and outrageous, that when God does answer them, God alone is the only logical explanation. God hears and answers every one of them. I am encouraged, and my faith is strengthened by every one of them.

I do not need to have my prayers answered, and I do not need to hear His voice. I see Him working every day, in my wife, my daughter, my friends, the church, even strangers.

My anchor is not dependent on how He treats me. His grace is sufficient. My anchor holds on a much larger scale.

The one prayer God has answered this year is my prayer to spend more time in prayer.

My purpose was reset. It has been re-developing ever since. Everyone's purpose begins with living one day at a time. Apparently, mine had a reset button. Over time your specific purpose will emerge. It will also change as the seasons of your life do.

Some Perspective on Significance

Not to repeat a thought, but purpose has been a very elusive concept for me over the years. There's a reason for that. Well there's always a reason for everything, but the light bulb is realizing it in your own life.

To know your purpose in life is an extremely powerful asset. Some never discover it in the first place. Too many people forget their purpose. Too many people get so caught up in the pursuit of money or power, career or basic survival, that they forget there's a why—a reason they're living.

> **Too many people get so caught up in living—or surviving—that they forget what they're living for.**

You have a purpose that is beyond you. You are called to something much greater than video games, weekend parties, or anything the media may throw at you.

Your purpose transcends your current situation. You are to live your purpose in your current and future work. You are to live your purpose in your home with your spouse and children. You are to live your purpose wherever you find yourself. When you truly know your purpose in life, you know it's not about you.

Why are you here?

Know your purpose in life, and you will know why you are here, in this place at this time. Forget your purpose, and you will feel lost and lose focus. And then money, greed, a thirst for power, or the need to survive will fill that void.

Consider the following concepts for finding (or re-finding) your purpose and letting it affect your daily life.

Live Each Day as If You Mean It

> *The purpose of life is a life of purpose.*
> Robert Byrne, an American author

This first idea is pointed and accurate. Every one of us needs to seek after our own purpose in life. I believe there are two types of purpose for each of us.

When Jesus was asked to pick the greatest commandment, He didn't give us one, but two commandments to embrace above all others.

> [28] *One of the teachers of the law came and heard them debating. Noticing that Jesus had given them a good answer, he asked him, "Of all the commandments, which is the most important?"*
>
> [29] *"The most important one," answered Jesus, "is this: 'Hear, O Israel: The Lord our God, the Lord is one.* [30] *Love the Lord your God with all your heart and with all your soul and with all your mind and with all your strength.'* [31] *The second is this: 'Love your neighbor as yourself.' There is no commandment greater than these."*
>
> Mark 12:28–31 NIV

I find purpose in these two commandments that stretches beyond personal achievement. I understand that not everyone reading this book agrees with the Bible. That is your choice. You may disagree with the very premise of the first commandment. But the second one is hard to dismiss, regardless of belief.

With the first, there is an overarching purpose for all mankind: glorify God in all we do. Whether you are a plumber or a CEO, an engineer or barista, it doesn't matter. What you do as a profession or trade is not what defines you as a person with this purpose; what defines you is that you glorify God in all you do.

The second is more specific to the individual, to you. That is: to help others. Whether you build structures, clean sewers, create online products, work for yourself or someone else, write, or perform skills of mind and skills of matter, all should be done with a sense of personal purpose guiding you. That purpose is to help others.

The greatest products in the world, from online courses to beautiful buildings, all are achievements of someone wishing to make other people's lives a little better.

See your purpose daily and your days will be filled. You will have no problem waking up every morning with an agenda, goals, to-do lists, and so on that coincide with your purpose.

If you wake up scratching your head at the day before you, you need to dive deep into the process of finding your own life purpose. One that is specific to you. One that encompasses and blends your known overarching purposes with your specific life plans.

Place Your Purpose First on Your Daily List

Put First Things First
Stephen Covey, 7 Habits of Highly Effective People

When you know your purpose, which drives your life goals and life plans, you are able to place tasks that advance your priorities at the top of your daily agenda.

In his teaching, Stephen Covey talks about big rocks. Those rocks are your most important things. If you take a jar and drop in too many little rocks and some sand, then try to put the big rocks in last, there's a very good chance they will not fit.

However, if you take the big rocks—your most important things—and put them in the jar first, they fit. Once those are in, you can add little rocks and sand around the big rocks. If some of the smaller ones don't fit, no big deal. However, if the big ones, the important ones, don't get in first, then there's a big problem, and you're spending too much time on the little things that don't matter.

In the book, *Organize Tomorrow Today*, by Dr. Jason Selk & Tom Bartow, the authors suggest eight skills necessary to accomplish the goal in the title. Their first suggested skill is to identify your three most important tasks for the next day. These three "must do" things, which should reflect your purpose, should be laid out in a practical plan that will ensure that at least some progress is made toward completion of these tasks. Here's the idea in a nutshell:

> *Write it out daily. Don't type it. Get a book, a journal, a planner. Make tomorrow's list before the end of the day, preferably before supper. Read your three tasks just before going to bed. Tackle the first task as soon as possible the next morning. Win early. Don't take a zero on any task. At worst, spend at least one minute on each task.*[5]

I've used several planners over the years, including creating my own à la the Bullet Journal[6] format. I'm currently using the Full Focus Planner created by Michael Hyatt. It's a quarterly planner that gives primary emphasis on focusing on and achieving your goals. I like it because, when used to its potential, it can keep your purpose in focus through writing out three main tasks for each day, based on goals you've set to achieve. Implementing it daily keeps my focus on goals that amplify my purpose.

What are your core priorities in your life, and how do they reflect your purpose? Can you formulate tasks that are driven by these priorities? How will these tasks become a part of your daily activity?

Find a Need and Meet It

The things which matter most must never be at the mercy of things which matter least.
Goethe, German Writer and Statesman

My very first week in ministry, fresh out of college with a shiny new degree, and I thought I knew everything in the world.

There was a guest speaker at the church that Sunday and it wasn't me. I can't for the life of me remember who it was. I remember she was female.

I was introduced to her after the service, and she congratulated me on being there, beginning a new ministry. Her one piece of advice to me was very simple: "Find a need and meet it."

At the time I thought it was terrible advice. I couldn't even begin to grasp what it even meant. I was ready for programming, special events, fun outings, and meaningful Bible studies. I was never taught to find and meet a need.

I was clueless.

Looking back, it was the best advice anyone ever gave me when it came to ministry. But it's more than that. It is a daily way of life. When you're meeting another person's needs you become relevant to that person. You become real, open, and honest with the world around you. You matter. You make a difference.

If you're still searching for your own purpose in life, make this a daily habit while you're searching. You'll find your own purpose more quickly.

Develop Unstoppable Clarity

Clarify daily your primary purpose in life.
Jonathan Milligan. Blogger who helps people

When you are sure, I mean sure, what your personal purpose in life is, nothing should be allowed to stand in your way. You need to become unstoppable in your quest: your journey to live out your purpose on this planet in your space at your time.

The more clearly and precisely you can verbalize your own purpose for your life, the more unstoppable you become.

Think bulldozer, not sports car. Sure, both can break down. I get that. Both have very different purposes for existence. Remember this: forces that can throw a sports car over a cliff or into a wall simply won't affect a bulldozer. A bulldozer is slow and heavy but extremely stable and focused in its ability and purpose. Having a bulldozer-like purpose will serve you better over the long term. Work at it slowly. Move forward every day.

You want your purpose to be bulldozer-like, steady, unstoppable, and narrow in focus. You're not trying to beat the competition. You're moving the obstacles out of your way.

In a recent interview with Kevin Monroe, founder of X Factor Consulting, he talked about having "mindset reminders" sent to him daily. He set these reminders up himself on his phone to remind him in different ways of his overall purpose in his work and life. Wonderful use of an iPhone, don't you think? He counted them up one day and found he had around twenty-three mindset reminders loading up his phone messages every day. When you think about it, it's better to have these reminders on your phone than ones that say,

"Amazon: Shipped your package..." and you wonder what your wife bought on your Prime account.

Mindset reminders are a great way to keep you on task, and your life purpose in focus. By the way, the low-tech equivalent would be post-it notes on your desk and bookshelf. Kevin had those as well.

You can listen to this interview on the *Coffee for Your Soul* Podcast, episode 026.[7]

Make Journaling a Daily Discipline

My wife and daughter started me down a path of journaling every day. My daughter has been journaling for years now, ever since high school.

Daily write about your life and your purpose.

I now journal every morning. Sometimes it is the most trivial of things. (My fantasy football quarterback sucked this past weekend.) Sometimes it's very introspective. (I couldn't shake my feelings of depression all day yesterday.) Sometimes it's celebratory. (Yay, Lisa and I are going away for the weekend.) It is whatever you write down. It is your journal. It is your life. And your life should reflect your purpose.

Journaling will help you focus on your life's purpose.

Some recommend using a template for journaling. What happened yesterday? What are your plans for today? Three things to be grateful for, and so on. Others, like me, write whatever comes to mind.

If you start every day by reinforcing your purpose in print and how you plan to go through the day living that purpose, it will end up being a great memory of a life lived on purpose.

My journal is electronic (Evernote app) and most of the time I take a picture of myself (yes, a selfie) that goes along with the day's entry. Someday, hopefully, many years from now, my daughter and her kids will want to remember me. They'll read my journal, see my picture, and laugh. They'll read of the silly things that happened to me, and they'll never mistake what my purpose in life was.

Have Friends with Similar Purpose

Nothing can kill a great day like hanging around with friends who are on a completely different "script" than you are. Sure, they may be friends, but their passions aren't your passion. Their goals in life are in a completely different direction than yours.

Surround yourself daily with friends of like purpose.

Find friends with similar life goals and purpose. Begin to brainstorm with each other about how to grow and strive toward fulfilling your similar purposes.

My daughter has a passion for missionary service. She always finds people to be around who will encourage her in her purpose and pursuits. You want to be around people who will prod you toward living your purpose, not pull you in a different direction.

I've dumped several Facebook friends in past years for this very reason. You know how Facebook friends are, I'm sure. Some are just there. Some you don't even know. Some are encouraging. Some are honest. Then there are some who have nothing good to say to you and have no problem voicing their opinion and sucking the energy out of you. These are the ones you need to stop following or drop altogether. Refuse to give any time or voice to doubters in your life.

Find friends who will get behind you and fill your sails with purpose. The wrong kind of friends don't fill your sails. They weigh down the boat. Some even try to sink it.

Keep Going Until You Know Where You're Headed

When driving at night, your headlights only shine so far out in front of you. To see farther down the road, you keep the vehicle moving in that direction. A stationary vehicle has limited vision simply because it's stationary.

Daily move forward with your life purpose.

If you're not completely sure of your purpose in your life, at least you have an idea or a general direction. Start moving in that general direction. Your vision of your purpose will become more clear as you inch closer.

Here's an example: I'm headed to Colorado. Okay, so go to Colorado. Where in Colorado? Denver appeals to me. Great. Where in Denver are you headed? I don't know yet. Let me get to Denver first, then I'll get more specific. Sounds great.

You don't need to be specific if you've never been there before. You move the car through the darkness to see farther down the road, or around the corner. There are times when the headlights show obstacles. Great. Drive around them, but keep moving forward.

Moving in the direction of your passion every day is one step closer to living a life of purpose. Specific goals become clearer as you move forward.

Giving is the Highest Form of Living

I believe I heard this first back in the late '70s from John Maxwell, author and motivational speaker. It has stuck with me ever since. I have never felt so personally fulfilled in any given moment than when I was able to give in some way to other people.

Give daily to needs that fit your passion and your purpose. Others need what you can give. You may even discover your purpose as you see needs in this world and give to help fill those needs.

Giving reminds you that you should not be the focus of your own life. We all have a purpose that is greater than ourselves. Everyone does. Look past yourself, and give your time, your talents, and your treasure to causes that fit your purpose. If you are so inclined, ask God to bless your gift and cause it to be multiplied.

One of the biggest mistakes you can make when plotting out your true purpose in life is to think that it will not affect, or be affected, by the lives of those around you. You have a higher calling in life than to only take care of you.

Always Begin Your Day with Purpose

Seriously, the first thing you do every day can have a huge impact on the tone of your entire day.

Feed your mind with purpose every morning.

My close friend starts his day, every day, by reading the Word of God before he anything else. This is what he wants to go into his heart and mind first thing every morning.

His choice to do so is reflective of his life's purpose. Notice I didn't say his vocation. He's an engineer who helped found and build a company. His vocation is not his purpose. His purpose is reflected in how he conducts himself in his vocation. His purpose is to honor God in His life.

Starting his day with Scripture helps him focus on his higher calling. It grounds him in his daily activities.

This may not be you, depending on your personal beliefs. If this is the case, start your day by putting something into your mind that positively reflects your purpose in life. Have something that kicks off your day. Make it personal. Make it yours.

What can you do first thing every morning that helps you focus on your life's purpose?

- Create a morning mantra.
- Queue something up on your smart phone to listen to.

- Develop a reading plan that motivates you and pulls you forward.

Whatever you can do to positively feed your purpose, find a way to start your day with it.

Be Proactive When Life Happens

Life happens a lot. The car breaks down. You get the flu. A huge traffic jam makes you late for your next appointment. Your cell phone battery dies, and you have no way of charging it. You lose your wallet. Your car has a flat tire. You leave a pen in your pocket, and it ruins your shirt in the wash. Always reacting to life is almost never fun.

Be ready daily to tweak your circumstances.

I want you to know something. I want you to say it out loud.

"It's going to be okay."

Now, breathe. Just breathe. If you can breathe, you can move forward. Tweak on the run. That's what I call it. Tweaking is adjusting to life without losing focus. It's taken me many years to realize that you must be proactive when life slaps you in the face or some other body part. You're much less likely to be angry and upset. However, if you must get upset, take a minute and be upset. When the minute is up, move on.

Whatever happens in life, look for the opportunity to live your purpose and be proactive with it. Get ahead of any disappointment and surprise. You tweak your day to fit the situation.

The trick is to tweak your day without losing sight of your purpose. This is a learned skill that takes some time to master. If it can be learned, it can be mastered.

Let God Lead You As You Live Your Purpose

God's purpose is more important than our plans.
Myles Munroe, Bahamian Minister

[I have no idea how this will translate to those of you reading who do not have God in your life. My purpose is not to crowd my "religion" into your life. Feel free to skip over these next few paragraphs if you feel this isn't for you. I understand.]

One of the biggest mistakes you can make when plotting out your true purpose in life is to think that it is supposed to be your life purpose.

My wife and I walk in the park several times a week, usually in the evening. For the first time in many months a homeless man was sitting on a park bench. I assume he was homeless, but I don't know for sure. He wasn't begging for food or money. He was just sitting there. Lisa and I walked on by, nodding polite greetings, and never breaking pace.

I couldn't shake the feeling that I was to do something for the man. The farther we walked away from him, the more I felt a nudge to give him something. I looked at Lisa and said, "I have to do this." And I did.

All I had in my wallet was my "emergency" $50 bill. We did a U-turn, and as we walked back by him, I stuck out my hand to shake his. As he complied with my greeting, I slipped the money to him. We kept on walking. I was nudged, prompted, to do something. Doing so reminded me of my purpose, our purpose: to be people who give.

When prompted, act. Be open to how God may lead you throughout the day. You may not yet have a clear understanding of your purpose, but He does.

Spend Your Time On Your Purpose

People who use time wisely spend it on activities that advance their overall purpose in life.
John C. Maxwell

Some people have very little discretionary time. Eight to ten-hour work days. Chores to do at home for the family. General maintenance on the house, the car, and so on.

A person with purpose guards his time. A person with purpose finds time to work on his purpose. Realize that time is the only commodity you can't get back. When a day is done, you will never get that day back. A person with purpose is always moving forward, even by small steps when life gets crazy. Long journeys are chipped away one day at a time.

There are many examples of people who became very successful with online businesses by finding and utilizing their spare time—two hours early in the morning or a few hours later in the evening. They found the time and used it productively. They knew that little steps taken each day will get them where they need to go.

Frame Your Day With Thankfulness

Every morning I wake up and thank God.
Aaron Neville, R&B singer

Aaron Neville frames his day with faith in God. That works for Aaron Neville. What works for you? No matter who you thank, be thankful.

Thankfulness is an amazing way to focus on a purpose greater than yourself. Just being thankful is a great way to spend any day, no matter how you frame it. Here are ways to start:

- Thankful for being able to frame your day in faith.
- Thankful for being alive
- Thankful for your spouse
- Thankful for the children you are raising
- Thankful for food to eat
- Thankful for friends who fill your sails
- Thankful for the pet in your life
- Thankful for the gift of learning
- Thankful for one more breath
- Thankful for one more cup of coffee (Hey, I like coffee)

The more thankful you are for everything around you, and the more you look around and be thankful, you frame your day in the faith.

WARNING: Don't be thankful you're better off than the next guy. Comparison is a guaranteed way to kill focus on your own purpose.

Live from the Knees Up

Prayer does not fit us for the greater works;
prayer is the greater work.
J. Oswald Sanders

I cannot exclude this short thought from the book because it is part of my own purpose. Again, and without apology, if the idea of faith isn't for you, that is your choice. Just skip to the next section.

I don't simply start my day in prayer. I make an effort to live my day in prayer. It's not as easy as it sounds. I can get so caught up in the "stuff" of the day that prayer is the last thing on my mind. But when I'm on my game:

- When I see something that isn't right, I pray about it.
- When I sense something that makes me feel awkward, I pray about it.
- When I begin to feel depressed or down on myself, I pray about it.

> PRAY DAILY.
> PRAY DELIBERATELY.
> PRAY DECIDEDLY.

We're not talking long, glorious, holy liturgy here. Just breathing a prayer to God about the situation. Doing this is fulfilling my God-ordained purpose of living to honor Him.

Part of my purpose is to see what needs to be prayed for. Keeping my eyes open to needs is a developing skill set. Breathing a simple prayer for the guy that cut me off in traffic is better than reacting with anger.

Remember, we do not know what others are going through in their lives that make them act the way they do. They need our prayers.

Focus Can Be Hard at Times

Focus is hard work. Fortunately, the more you work at it, the better you get at it. Focus is what you do in work and in life to keep the idea of life purpose before you. Here are seven areas of focus you can begin to work on daily.

SPIRITUAL
Focus daily on your relationship with God
through prayer and the Scriptures.

SELF-DEVELOPMENT
Focus daily on becoming a better you.
Feed your mind with positivity.

FAMILY
Focus daily on loving your family
with your time, attention, and trust.

CAREER
Focus daily on advancing your vocation
with integrity and hard work.

FINANCES
Focus daily on making money and spending less
so you can save more and give more.

PHYSICAL
Focus daily on healthy living
with regular exercise and smart consumption.

SOCIAL
Focus daily on building community with
people who you can support, and from whom you
can receive support.

**Which Brings Us Back to the Reason
We All Need Purpose**

With a good sense of purpose hanging over your head and seeping into your heart and mind, I want you to shift your focus to achieving something aligned with that purpose.

The Bigger Picture of Purpose

It doesn't matter what you achieve so long as it reflects your purpose in some way.

Perhaps this "future achievement" will inspire you to an even bigger challenge or inspire someone else to chase their own life achievement. Either way, let's get at it. Let's go **There**.

In Okinawa, there are more people who live beyond a 100-year-old than anywhere else in the world. There, they do not have a word for "retirement." They have an ikigai. In a 2001 research paper on ikigai, co-author Akihiro Hasegawa, a clinical psychologist and associate professor at Toyo Eiwa University, placed the word ikigai as part of everyday Japanese language. It is composed of two words:

iki, which means life, and *gai*, which describes value or worth.

There was a very old man who lived in Okinawa who was close to, if not, over a 100-year-old. One of his exercises every day was cutting grass. He used an old-fashioned, one-handed sickle. This activity had several outcomes. First, the grass had to be cut. He cut a certain amount each day. Second, by doing so he got exercise every day. This was a healthy practice. Finally, he didn't cut only his own grass. Others needed long grass cut as well. He was helping others. He had a reason to get up every day.

Ikigai essentially is the reason why you get up in the morning.

Your ikigai is the bridge between the first and the second question. You've read about purpose in life, and now you need to translate that idea into a more concrete, doable activity. The second question challenges you to set a goal before you and pursue that goal.

4

THE GIFT OF GOAL SETTING

What do you want?

The secret of getting ahead is getting started.
The secret of getting started is breaking your complex
overwhelming tasks into small manageable tasks,
and starting on the first one.
Mark Twain

Kaizen is another Japanese word, defined as "continuous improvement." In business, it is a strategy where employees at all levels of a company work together proactively to achieve regular, incremental improvements to the manufacturing process. In a sense, it combines the collective talents within a company to create a powerful engine for improvement.

Let's not get too deep here. Consider the idea that kaizen is part action plan and part philosophy. Kaizen as an action plan is exactly what develops kaizen as a philosophy.

The idea of "continuous improvement" in your own life is why you set goals and work daily to achieve them. Change for the better, and then continuously improve the process.

I have a morning routine that you will read about eventually. I haven't always done this. This is how it is now. Having a morning routine (specific habits working together) was a change for the better in my life. It took me at least six months of tweaking and adjusting to get it the way it is right now. It won't stay that way. At some point, it will need to be tweaked again. Adjustment is part of the progress.

What do you want?

As I write this chapter, the playoffs are on. I don't watch the regular season at all, just the playoffs. The playoffs are much more intense. It's win four or go home. They do that four times to win it all. Best four out of seven, four times.

The worst-case scenario is to play seven games, losing three of those seven, winning the seventh, and moving on to play seven games, losing three of those seven, winning the seventh, and moving on to play seven games, losing three of those seven, winning the seventh, and moving on to play seven final games, losing three of those seven, yet winning the seventh and final game to become the champions. That's twenty-eight games. Like I said, worst case scenario. I'm tired just reading it. A little dizzy as well.

By the way, I'm talking about hockey, the NHL (National Hockey League). I grew up in a small town in Canada where hockey was the only sport we cared about. There was curling, but we didn't care about curling. Simple sport, hockey. Put the puck in their net more times than the other guys, within a designated time limit. Do it enough times, and you get the trophy. Enough times means more than the other guys.

At the beginning of every season every team has the same goal in mind: win the Stanley Cup. Win the trophy. Thirty teams all with the same final goal. Twenty-nine will be disappointed.

Any of the twenty-nine teams could have won the Kelly Cup. What is the Kelly Cup, you ask? The trophy for the champion of the East Coast Hockey League, the minors. Completely unchallenging to an NHL team. Completely unfair to everyone else in the ECHL. For most of us, though, trying out for the ECHL would be crazy (and a little bit dangerous!).

You're not playing hockey. You're going **There**. How far away should your **There** be? Your **There**, not someone else's **There**. Their **There** shouldn't matter to you. Got it? Hope so.

Your **There** should be far enough so that when you get **There** (and you WILL get **There**) you'll know you've accomplished something extraordinary in your life.

Not extraordinary to anyone else's life, only to your life. Your life is not a competition with the Jones's or whoever your neighbors are. Your competition is between you being Here and getting **There**.

How far? Far enough to be hard. Far enough to get you out of your comfort zone. Far enough to mean something to you. Far enough to be significant to you and only you. No one else.

Defining your **There** should be intimately connected to your overall purpose in life. Now, I know what you're thinking, I think. You're thinking, "How was your climbing a volcano intimately connected to your overall purpose, Bill? Hmmm? What about that?"

Good question. Here's my best answer: Climbing that volcano got me out of a rut. It got me out of a chair. It got me out of the house. It sparked my long-lost sense of adventure. It got me going again. Doing it reminded me of a greater purpose in my life, one I never should have set on the shelf to collect dust. It got me living again. It got me believing in doing other things like writing this book and starting a podcast. It got me blogging again. It got me off the bench, and back into the game.

My purpose slowly became diluted in the mundane, the rut of living. It faded over time. It slowly became misplaced somewhere along my timeline. That volcano sparked something in me to get going again. Climbing that volcano renewed my purpose.

Hope that answers your question somewhat. Your **There**, your goal, needs to be something that gets you to do the things that my **There** did for me—and more.

Defining your **There** needs some structure. Inspiration may be the lightbulb, but the infrastructure to get that light on requires a lot of wiring, or at least a fully charged battery or two.

Have you ever tried to retrofit a AAA battery to work in a AA socket? (Is socket the right word here? Not sure, but you know what I mean.) Maybe you have. How'd that work out for you? Not so good, I'd guess. It can be done, but it's not the ideal long-term solution.

One of the best things you can do when challenged to leave your Here and go **There** is to have a clear knowledge of exactly where **There** is. Don't settle for retrofitting someone else's **There**. AA-sized sockets are only ideal for AA batteries. Individuality matters.

Specificity is your first step to getting **There**.

Which would you consider the better statement for me on my volcano quest?

- I will climb a volcano.
- I will climb a volcano in Guatemala.
- I will climb Volcán Acatenango in Guatemala.
- I will go to Guatemala and climb to the top of Volcán Acatenango on June 29, 2014.

Each statement becomes more specific. Specificity is the best way to clearly define a goal. I could have headed to Guatemala and stepped foot on the base of Acatenango, turned around, and gone home, having accomplished a goal that wasn't quite specific enough. No. You be specific enough so that when you've finally reached that goal, it is clear not only to you but also to everyone who knew your goal.

The Gift of Goal Setting

The more specific you are about your goals, the better and more able you'll be to accomplish them no matter what method you use. This means that you don't just say you want to make more money or lose more weight, you have to say exactly how much money you want to make or how much weight you want to lose. You have to put a real and exact figure on it.

Wanderlust Worker [blog post]

I stood on the top of Volcán Acatenango on June 29, 2014, and took a picture, a selfie, of me accomplishing my goal. Then I had someone else take a better picture of me. Proof of accomplishment. Proof of a goal conquered. I was **There**.

Acatenango is 13,045 feet above sea level. I've been higher, but that's not the point. Acatenango was my goal.

If you want to get There, define in detail exactly what you want to do.

It took over six hours on the first day, and over another hour in the dark on the second day to get there. It took changing my diet for four months prior and losing thirty-six pounds. It took ten thousand steps every day for over four months to prepare. I measured every bit of it. (Thank you, Fitbit.) I had defined **There** to the point that when I was **There**, I knew it.

Had my goal been, "I'm going to climb a volcano." I may still be thinking about which one to climb, and when.

In Antigua, Guatemala, I used an expedition company called OX. It's a hostel, an expedition/adventure organizer, and so on. When I committed to getting **There**, to the top of Acatenango, I contacted them. They were happy to make a reservation for me and take my money. They asked me my age, and I told them. I was fifty-five at the time. Then they tried to talk me out of doing it. They almost refused my application due to my age. I guess they were afraid I might have a heart attack on the way up. I assured them I was preparing properly for the adventure ahead.

They tried on the phone, and they tried the day before we left. They requested I come in and talk to them about it. I wasn't about to let them refuse me. I ended up signing a Release of Liability form, releasing them from any responsibility in case I expired somewhere along the route. (Spoiler #1: Everyone signed the same form, they made a big deal out of it for me due to my age. Spoiler #2: They let me go, *and* I didn't die.)

My getting **There** was achievable. It wasn't beyond my reach or ability. It was a challenge, but it wasn't impossible.

I've never dunked a basketball in my life. Not on a regulation height rim. Not even with a trampoline. I wasn't going **There**. That wasn't my **There** anyway. Dunking a basketball for a 5'9" white guy from Hockeyville, Canada, is beyond the boundaries of achievability for me. Not going to happen.

Sure, I could choose to try and go **There**. Get a trainer to teach me proper jumping technique, lift weights, build muscle, and so on. I'd put money on the fact that doing all of that *and* adding a trampoline would probably get me injured.

It's not just the lift. I'm somewhat uncoordinated. I'd have to work on timing. Some things can't be taught, and coordination like that may not be something I can learn. I would never be able to grip a basketball well enough to dunk.

Oh, one more thing: I don't want to dunk a basketball.

Despite the fact that it'd be cool for a guy my age to dunk a basketball on a public court in front of a bunch of middle schoolers, I still have no real passion to do so. Going **There** is therefore not achievable. Not for me.

Dunking at my age is not very relevant either. One could argue that climbing a volcano wasn't relevant either, but it was. I've already mentioned that.

Relevance goes back to your purpose in life. You define where your **There** is and work hard to get **There**. The main fuel for your daily grind from Here to **There** is your purpose. Your purpose sent power to a lightbulb over your head and

The Gift of Goal Setting

flicked the switch, illuminating **There** for you. The connection may not be obvious at first, but if you head **There,** you will see it in due time.

Speaking of time, when did I climb that volcano you're already sick of hearing about? June 29, 2014. Right. Five months prior, I had that date nailed down. That was my finish line, my acme-of-accomplishment, my trophy-on-top-of-the-podium date. It was the end of Here, and the culmination of **There**.

It is extremely important for you to know when you're going to arrive **There**. Saying something like, "Next year I'll be **There**," is a recipe for not getting there. It's too vague. January? Sometime in July, perhaps?

When you leave it too open like that, you find yourself in late December scrambling to get **There**, only to realize you're still too far away to achieve it.

Having a deadline, a big red circle on a date on a calendar, makes getting **There** seem more tangible, direct . . . what's the word . . . precise. You want to be precise.

With precision comes the ability to map your journey from Here to **There**.

I want to go to New York City. Great. Let's go. I hit the edge of the metropolis, and see a sign that says, "Welcome to New York City." Hey, I've arrived. Where's the Statue of Liberty? Where's the Empire State Building? Why can't I see that big bull staring at that little girl staring back at that big bull? My goal of getting **There** wasn't precise enough.

Precision is a serious matter in most of our modern world. And precision deals mostly with time.

The sign that said, "Welcome to New York City," also had a time frame attached to it. Let's say you're twenty miles from the sign. And it's going to take you forty minutes to get there. Traffic, right? Exactly. But from the sign to the bull staring at the girl is another twenty miles and it's going to take you about four hours to get to that exact spot. Traffic, right? Yes, traffic. Lots and lots of traffic. Too much traffic. Crazy traffic.

Attaching a time limit to your arrival **There** will change your method of getting **There**.

I went to New York one time to meet my sister. My goal was to meet my sister in New York and spend some time together. Had I said, "See you on Tuesday," I would have been met with, "Which Tuesday? Where and when?" Precision matters.

She was coming from Massachusetts. I was coming from Colorado. I flew into Newark, grabbed a train to Grand Central, and walked around for four hours until she got there. This was my plan. I walked around, got my bearings, checked out a few spots. Sis made it to the meeting spot on the preplanned day and time. I was there to greet her.

Precision matters. Timing matters. When you know your target finishing point, your plans to get **There** all point to that time frame.

With this planning laid out before you, determine a specific measurable outcome. It should be well within your capabilities as an achievable endeavor, and you should have your sights set on a relevant, worthwhile quest that reaches beyond, ya know, *you*. Set the deadline and . . .

Maybe you need to write this down. I think that'd be the smart thing to do. Writing something like this down on paper will keep your target literally in your face in a very unforgettable way.

This will help—a well-known acronym. Maybe it's new to you, but I've read more than a few articles, courses, and books that outline this concept for your goals. I became very interested in the process of using SMART goal-setting when I took a course first offered in December 2013 called *5 Days to Your Best Year Ever* offered by Michael Hyatt.[8]

I covertly mentioned each element of the **SMART** goals while telling you about climbing that blasted volcano.

- **Specific.** I will go to Guatemala and climb to the top of Volcán Acatenango on June 29, 2014. That is specific.

- **Measurable.** The location, the altitude, the route, the preparation, all of it was an exercise in measurement for me. The achievement was verified by photos, witnesses, and the amount of ash I kept having to dump out of my hiking boots. Very annoying.

- **Attainable.** Despite the guides who tried to talk me out of it, I proved it was attainable for me. No one else's opinion mattered since it was my goal, and no one else's.

- **Relevant.** It got me going again. It made me active. It sparked something within me that got me off my butt and challenged me. I needed that challenge at that time in my life. Relevance is specific to the individual. My volcano climb may never be relevant to you, but it was to me.

- **Time-Bound.** I set the date. I was only going to be in Guatemala for eighteen days. This was a two-day affair. I paid the money. I committed to these dates. I even left a buffer for the following weekend in case of bad weather or Fuego acting up again.

While doing research for this book, I came across a YouTube video by author and motivational speaker, Brendon Burchard. He kind of went off on not liking the SMART goal acronym. I still can't tell if he was totally serious or not. Either way, he offered another acronym in its stead—DUMB goals.[9]

- **Dream-Driven or Destiny-Driven.** This will be the break from being measurable to being way out there.

Nothing wrong with that at all. This is where the innovators/discoverers live and breathe. They refuse to accept doing what everybody else is doing. "Lose weight" anybody can do that. Restate it and it shifts to become "amazingly fit." Make it a gain and not a loss. I get it. Dream big. Make the goal worth the effort.

- **Uplifting.** Have a goal that is personally attractive to you. It is compelling and important. A goal that is positive in nature, and challenges you to act to reach that goal.

- **Method-Friendly.** A map if you will. Practices can be created around this goal that will make it easier to pursue. Create a set of practices that you repeat, over and over and over again. For me, these are the routines that pull the habits together and organize them for effective use.

- **Behavior-Driven.** Triggers set up to make you work toward your goal. For me, these are the cues that activate the habits. No cue—no behavior—no habit. No habits—no goal reached.

I agree with Brendon. I also agree with Michael. I do not see a conflict between these two acronyms and the truth they offer to you. DUMB goals spark your creativity and force you to dream outside the box. SMART goals, and the structure this acronym offers, could arguably fit within the idea of Burchard's Method-Friendly third point.

In the past few years, I've learned how to use a firearm safely. I've taken some courses and earned my concealed carry permit. I've even had the opportunity to learn from an ex-special ops veteran. (Never carry a gun like TJ Hooker. There's video of me making this mistake. By design, there is no link to this video.)

The Gift of Goal Setting

Starting out, everything I knew about guns I'd learned from Ziva David from the TV show NCIS. Not the best way to learn about firearms. From Ziva I learned that it's possible to be surgical with a firearm. By that I mean extremely accurate. Yes, I know it's a TV show, yet it's still completely possible.

From the real world, and from an ex-special ops army veteran, I learned better basic habits. I might add at this point, that this person enters 3-Gun competitions on a regular basis, winning more than losing. It's fun to watch him shoot. His instruction trumps Ziva's.

Learning proper aim was one of the first things he taught me. Focusing on the target is one of the things I needed to learn.

Focus on where you want the bullet to strike. This is not a general idea. This is a specific idea. You don't aim in the general vicinity of the target, you aim at the target. Well, that's not right either. You aim at a single point on the target. You aim at the bullseye.

What did Mel Gibson say in the movie, *The Patriot*, when instructing his boys how to shoot at the British? "Aim small. Miss small." What does that mean? I asked the internet. Here's the best concise answer:

> *It means that if you take your time and aim accurately at a small area of the target—like the bullseye on a paper target ("aim small")—then any inaccurate shot will obviously not hit the bullseye, but chances are it will still hit somewhere on the intended target ("miss small").*
>
> [unknown]

This is why you need to define exactly where your **There** is. Writing your **There** down on paper is the same as having a paper target with a bullseye you desperately want to hit.

Write down your goal, your bullseye. Then rewrite it again and again. Each time tweak it, refine it, sharpen it. Dial it in to razor-sharp focus. This is where I suggest you use a template that incorporates the SMART elements.

DUMB gets you dreaming and gives your dream legs. SMART sets out the steps those legs need to take, honing your goal into a bullseye on a target that you know you will hit.

Although there's a huge panorama in life, your focus should be set on one single thing. Sure, the vista may be breathtaking, but if your aim is to hit one single little rock you must ignore the grand views.

So, while you sit, write, and pinpoint your **There**, let's look at it from a slightly different angle. Trust me. It will help you focus. And focus is what you need if you do indeed plan to leave Here and start heading **There**.

Knowing why you want to go **There** is important. In the concept of a life-long dream, many details may be clear to you. Swinging in a hammock between two palm trees looking out on the ocean as the sun sets, sipping an exotic alcoholic beverage which includes a tiny umbrella, without a care in the world is an amazing dream. I want to go **There**.

Is it California? Florida perhaps? Oh wait. A Caribbean island. Yes! Which one? Cuba? (Probably not, but maybe.)

This dream of yours is not yet measurable. Nothing wrong with that at all. Remember, this is where the innovators and discoverers live and breathe. They refuse to accept doing what everybody else is doing. "Go to the beach." Anybody can do that. Your beach is still way out there across the water somewhere. You don't want just any beach. You want that one beach. Restate your dream. Become amazingly specific. Make it a positive experience, and keep any thought of bad weather away.

Such dreams can become very uplifting. That's what dreams should be. Whenever you think of it, picture it as your refined goal. Make it as attractive to you as the first time you thought of it. See it as compelling—a high priority.

The Gift of Goal Setting

It is a daily, positive statement of **There**. You know exactly what **There** looks like. It excites you with the idea that you will be **There**.

As already stated, getting **There** needs a plan, a map, a blueprint. Very few people head out into the unknown without a plan in mind.

Columbus never had a detailed map. The maps of his day showed the Orient east of Spain, around Africa, past India. He planned to do something no one had ever done before. He headed west into the complete unknown, but at least he had a plan, a goal of finding a better way to reach the Orient. He also had a method—a proven method. Ships with sails and experienced crews. Guys that knew how to sail. Men who'd already been at sea, and come back again. These sailing skills were repeated daily allowing him to get closer to being There. Day after day. Heading in a predetermined direction.

Columbus is a terrible example of setting a goal. Or is he? He was dream-driven, that's for sure. The thought of success was very uplifting. He talked a queen into financing three ships heading west, going where no man had gone before. He convinced three full crews to join him. His goal was very uplifting. The concept was method-friendly. Everybody on the trip knew how to sail. The thought of open water was not a deterrent to their voyage. Their daily activities, while on the ships, were behavior-driven. Yes, they were. They got up every morning and did their chores, mopped the decks, trimmed the sails, looked to the horizon. Everyone had their duties. If they stopped doing their part in sailing the ships, the ships would never have discovered the new world. Not what they had in mind initially, but you get the point.

DUMB got Columbus heading west.

SMART, however, got Kon Tiki to the South Pacific. Note the differences.

The 1947 Kon Tiki Expedition comprised a small team of Scandinavian adventurers led by Thor Heyerdahl. They had no nautical history of attempting similar endeavors either together or separately. Together they planned an expedition to prove that natives from the west coast of South America could have been the early settlers of Polynesia. How's that for being specific?

The distance they were looking at traveling was 4,300 miles. Quite measurable as they knew what they were getting into. They fashioned a craft made of balsa wood, typical of boats used hundreds of years earlier. They stocked it with the food and equipment needed. They did all the necessary calculations.

They saw their voyage as attainable, yet bordering on the edge of disaster if they failed. It was only relevant to proving a theory, but that's the point.

Thor wanted to prove his theory, and this was the only way he could do it. Picking the best time of year to begin—late April, the 28th to be exact—they set sail with an expected arrival time of late summer. That was the best they could do, considering this endeavor had never been recorded before. They would either complete the journey or disappear forever.

The expedition was an eventual success. You can see the elements of setting and defining the goal throughout the initial stages of the expedition. The success was in achieving such a goal.

You have this dream of achieving a goal in your life. It is uplifting and motivational in and of itself, utilizing a method that's proven and reliable. All you need to do is go after your goal.

Write your goal on a piece of paper. Just write it any way you want. Get it out there. Now you are ready to start!

Work your way through the SMART acronym to refine your goal.

- Is it SPECIFIC? Are there numbers or dates involved in this goal?

- Is it MEASURABLE? When you're done, how will you know? How will others know?

- Is it ATTAINABLE? Don't doubt yourself or sell yourself short. Do you remember Susan Boyle's first audition on *Britain's Got Talent*? (Google that. It's amazing.)

- Is it RELEVANT? How does this goal reflect your greater purpose?

- Is it TIME-BOUND? Does it have an end date or a finish line? How will you know when you're **There**?

Work on crafting your goal into a single statement that reflects this SMART framework. Doing this is the first real step to setting yourself up to succeed.

But I one other question to ask you: Why? Why do you want to go up that volcano? Why do you want to find a better route to the West Indies? Why do you want to prove that Peruvians may have settled in Polynesia? Why?

Once you've settled on chasing a big goal in your life, and before you go any further, you need to answer the Why question. The answer to this question is what will keep you going when you are tempted to quit.

5

THE MEASURE OF IDENTIFYING MOTIVES

Why do you want to go there?

"If I can't win, I won't run." Harold
"If you don't run, you can't win." Sybil
From the movie, *Chariots of Fire*

Harold Abrahams lost only one race his entire life. Only one. That race haunted him for the rest of his life.

That's the way the movie depicts it. *Chariots of Fire* is a 1981 movie starring Ian Charleson and Ben Cross. Ian played the role of Eric Liddell, a devout Christian called to missionary work in China, who happened to run very fast. Ben played Harold Abrahams who fought every day to shake the self-imposed stigma that he was a Jew. He, too, was very fast.

Both had to answer the question: why run? Why? There has to be a reason.

For Eric Liddell:

"I believe that God made me for a purpose. For China. But he also made me fast. And when I run I feel his pleasure. To give it up would be to hold Him in contempt."

Eric Liddell ran to honor God and the gift he was given. For Harold Abraham:

"Sybil: (about running) Do you love it?
  Harold: I'm more of an addict. It's a compulsion with me, a weapon I can use.
  Sybil: Against what?
  Harold: Being Jewish, I suppose.
  Sybil: [laughs incredulously] You're not serious! People aren't like that, people don't care. Can it be as bad as all that?
  Harold: You're not Jewish, or you wouldn't have had to ask.
  ... I'm forever in pursuit, and I don't even know what I'm pursuing."

Harold Abrahams ran in pursuit of self-justification.

Harold Abrahams lost only one race in his life. He lost to Eric Liddell. Two men doing the same thing very well. Both won gold medals at the 1924 Olympics. Two men ran for very different reasons, very different motives.

Both ran. Both went **There**.

Why do you want to go There?

Seriously. Why do you want to go **There**?

There's got to be a reason or two or ten. Why do you want to start now? Will the effort be worth it? Is the payoff big enough? Is it worth all this planning? Is it worth the daily grind? Is it worth the stretch? What about all the extra work or money involved?

What if you fail to get **There**? What about that, eh? Can you see yourself getting close but coming up short? Can you envision running that marathon and never crossing the finish line? Can you see yourself climbing up that mountain but never planting your flag on the peak?

We're not talking about your *What* anymore. We're talking about your *Why*.

Why?

Because, without a great Why, What won't happen. Without a great Why, **There** is a dream without drive (yawn). Without several great reasons Why, **There** may stay beyond your reach.

Having a **There** without knowing your Why will keep you from progress that's worth the effort.

When someone stops you on the street, gets in your face with bad breath, and questions you with a loud, raspy voice, why you need to have an answer. You have lots of answers. You rattle them off to him as loud, probably louder.

You need to silence the doubters in your life. Who are they to say you can't go **There**? Who do they think they are, telling you to stop this silly quest of yours.

They may even tell you they've been **There** and it's no big deal. It's not worth the time, effort, and money involved. Of course, you know they're lying, don't you? How could they ever have been **There**, since it's your **There** and not theirs?

And then there's the effort itself that tells you to stop. Yes, the effort itself. Ever go for a run in the rain? I haven't, but many do. I'll guarantee every one of them, at some point during the run, asked themselves, "Why am I doing this?" They're cold, wet, and haven't had coffee yet, but they're out there running. Why? Because they've already answered the Why question.

They answered it before heading out the door. They answered it before even putting on their running shoes. When you answer the Why before your daily effort toward **There**, you are no longer intimidated by the task itself.

You may already be sick of the volcano story so here's one about a mountain.

It took me two attempts to get to the top of Long's Peak. Two tries. Passing me were teenage girls and 75-year-old men. The first time up, I couldn't catch my breath.

The first time, I was with my good friend Tim, his son Matthew, and his son-in-law, Nathan. Tim and I are about the same age. I went along for the ride because it was a good opportunity for me to hang out with good people, good friends, and go to the top of something impressively high. We had no plan. Honestly. In fact, up until 8:00 p.m. the night before, we were planning a completely different hike. One that would have required our wives to pick us up at the other end, which was two hours from home. They were not on board with that interruption of their weekend. Therefore, we chose a different hike.

From the Long's Peak trailhead to the Boulder Field, by way of the Keyhole route, it is slightly over five and a half miles with 3,825 feet in elevation change. The Keyhole is a little over 13,000 feet elevation. From there to the top of Long's Peak is one and a half miles with another 1,200 feet in elevation change, topping out at 14,259 feet. It's a climb, and I'd never done anything like it before.

Off we went. I was the slowest hiker in the group, but I was determined not to keep the group from keeping a good pace. That never happened. By the time we got to the Boulder Field, I was gassed. I had water and food, but I couldn't catch my breath.

Getting from the Boulder Field to the Keyhole (about a quarter of a mile) took me about half an hour. I had no energy. I had no lung capacity. I had no explanation for it. Fortunately, I hadn't lost my common sense.

The young guys had already gone on ahead. Tim was full of energy and ready to catch them. Not me. I had the sense to recognize that on this day, I wasn't going any further. The Keyhole was my stopping point. I asked Tim what was ahead, and he didn't know. It was his first time there. We'd both read about the last part of the route. It has the hardest non-technical climb in the state. It has its risks, with steep routes, ledge traverses, and over 1,200 feet of elevation in one and a half miles of hiking/climbing. You need to have your wits about you if you're going to do it. If only I were 30 years younger, but I wasn't.

Young people decide on a whim to do this hike. Older people prepare and do it. I was in the middle. I had little planning and little preparation, but I was going to give it a shot anyway. The lack of breath without any good explanation for it forced me to decide. Stop at the Keyhole, or forge ahead regardless.

What was I going to do? What should I do? Why should I do it?

I talked briefly with Tim who was torn between staying with me or going ahead to be with his sons. I told him to get on with it. I wasn't alone at the Keyhole. Dozens of people were either going up or coming back down. I had food and water. It was a gorgeous day. The only thing I lacked was oxygen. My decision to wait was based on that fact alone. There was no reason to continue if I couldn't catch my breath.

I called it a day at the Keyhole. I decided to stop. I chose to wait until a more opportune time. So I took time to rest. I caught my breath over the next thirty minutes and took my time descending from the Keyhole back down through the boulder field. Then I put my feet up and relaxed.

Over an hour later, probably closer to two, the other three found me. They had reached the top. They had seen and experienced what I had chosen not to, experienced what I could not, and hiked and climbed what I had no breath to attempt.

The rest of the hike was all downhill from there. Literally downhill. I was rested, and they were much more tired. Tim tried to convey to me every part of the trip that I hadn't experienced. He described the rest of the trail, the steepness of different turns and obstacles. He shared with me the final stretch to the top. The top, by the way, is flat. It's a little bigger than a football field. The wind is constant. That makes sense. It's over 14,000 feet high—14,259 feet to be exact. There's an official marker on a rock indicating that height. They had seen it. I hadn't. I took their word for it.

At first, I was quite discouraged that I couldn't continue. I felt defeated and conquered by a mountain. It wouldn't be the first time someone stopped at that spot and turned around. It wouldn't be the last. I hate quitting. It goes against my instincts.

After about fifteen minutes of feeling like a failure, I reassessed the situation. It wasn't a competition. It wasn't a race. It wasn't a he-man contest to see who was better. I felt at the time that my decision was not rash, rushed, or wrong. It was my decision, and mine alone. Tim wanted me to continue but understood why I didn't. He didn't try to force my hand. I sent him on quickly so he'd have time on top with his boys.

I was happy for them, but I knew I'd be back. I knew my time had not expired on this adventure, this challenge. I would get to the peak, even though teenage girls and retirees, probably hundreds of them, would do so on a moment's notice. It was not a competition. Not with them, anyway. It was a competition with myself.

Not reaching the top on the first attempt was the beginning of answering my Why question.

The second time I was a little more prepared. When approached again by Tim, to give it another try, I was ready. Sort of.

Believe it or not, I was about fifty days into the P90X exercise program. (The guy who started that program is a sadist.) I had built up some muscle and some cardio. This became part of my eventual success, but it wasn't the primary reason for it. This time, before we left, days before we left, I told myself, and no other, that I wasn't coming down until I reached the very top. My mind was made up before we ever got close to the mountain. This was something I did not do on my first attempt.

That previous attempt was a hike in the woods with some friends. This time it was a personal challenge to get **There,** and nothing was going to stop me.

Tim was invited by two work associates. One was on track to finish climbing all fifty-three peaks in Colorado. Truly he is a manly man. Ironically, this was his second attempt at Long's Peak, just like me. Hmm, something in common. On his first attempt, he brought his dog along. A National Park ranger made him descend before the Boulder Field because dogs weren't allowed on the trail. I had no "dog excuse" from my first attempt. That's okay. I had plenty of other excuses.

There was a fourth hiker with us who was a novice at hiking, even less at climbing. Long's Peak was going to be his first long, hard trek. Good for him.

Here's a quick recap. Tim's been to the top once already. Manly-man was on his second ascent. The novice had little clue but went along for the challenge. Me? Well you already know about me.

We were at the trailhead at 3:00 a.m. The trailhead parking lot was already full. We ended up parking about a mile away. That's adding more mileage to a day when we didn't need it. Up we went.

I felt good. Amazingly good. P90X gave me confidence and stamina. The real test was ahead of us. I knew I could reach the boulder field. I'd been there before. Good place for a rest. My breathing was good. I wasn't gassed. Let's get at it.

It's amazing where people get their confidence. Here are three examples:

> Tim: He's already been there. I'm feeding off the confidence of being with someone of previous experience.

Manly Man: Although he's never been to the top of Long's Peak, he has been to the top of more 14er's than the rest of us combined. He exudes confidence, and everyone feeds off this guy's energy.

The Novice: He's slower than me. If it was a race, I'm sure I could beat him. Instead of me being the slow, pokey guy, he was. I wasn't the tag-along. He was. Sadly, that gave me a little bit of confidence. Ego confidence. Comparison confidence. My apologies.

From the Boulder Field, things changed drastically. A hike became a climb. Steep turned steeper. Wind got stronger. Vertigo was more apparent. Fear of heights showed up in force. That was me from that point on. Little did I realize, until this point, that stopping on my first attempt was a very wise thing to do. Continuing was a bad idea for anyone who was out of energy and gassed at the boulder field. But on this day, I wasn't stopping until I got to the top—until I got **There**.

Why? Because as soon as I said yes to Tim when he asked me to join him, I also said yes to completing it this time. This time, failure was not an option. There was no turning around, turning back, or getting gassed. There was no excuse this time. My 100% commitment kicked in the moment I said yes. This was weeks before we left, before I put my hiking boots on, and before I packed a single bag of trail mix.

Commitment happens before the event, not during the event or after the event.

Commitment happens in the den, in front of a TV playing a DVD of some guy telling you to do one more set of fifteen reps of an exercise you absolutely hate before starting on the next set of exercises you also hate.

Commitment happens when you dismiss every excuse as invalid and unacceptable. "But what if . . . ?" "How about . . . ?"

Commitment is having an answer that's bigger and stronger than the "why?"

What would keep me from this climb? Well, if I seriously sprained my ankle because the P90X guy was too gung-ho and overly motivational (he is), then I'd have to postpone things. Or, if the weather called for severe thunderstorms, then it's probably not a good idea to stand tall while being that close to the heavens and targeted thunderbolts. (Oh, for a two-iron. Old golfing joke.) The rain would make the rocks nearly impossible to navigate. So, some outside factors could derail or postpone the plans. Apart from that, onward and upward.

Past the boulder field was all rock ledges and ascension. Tim was leading, but there was no reason for him to do so. We were not alone on this rock. It was a Saturday. Remember the parking lot. Teenage girls were doing this hike. Families conquered it together. Runners. Seriously, runners were motoring up and down like it was a walk in the park. Well, it is a walk in the park, but the park is a very serious one.

Up we went.

As I recall, we'd go around for a while, then take an upward turn to a climb. Around some more, and then a climb. You couldn't see beyond the semi-horizontal round or beyond the near-vertical climbs. Remember, Long's Peak is known as the hardest non-technical 14er in Colorado. Therefore, no harnesses or ropes were necessary, although many times I wish I'd been strapped in. Did I mention my fear of heights? (I blame my ten-meter tower incident. That story's a few chapters ahead.)

False hope is still hope, isn't it? I started to get gassed again, but I wasn't stopping. Since Tim had been up this monster once before, I kept asking him what any five-year-old would ask on a long car trip: "Are we there yet?" "How much further?" "I have to pee." Okay, I didn't say that last one, but I did repeatedly ask him the first two. He kept saying,

"Just a little further, I think." "Just up the next ascension, I'm sure." "The last slope up is just ahead." He must have said these phrases five times. Maybe more. It kept me going. He wasn't completely sure, and that's okay. The point is, it kept me going.

Somewhere along the last one and a half-mile rock climb, we met two men. I think it was a father and son. Maybe a grandfather and grandson. In either case the older of the two was in his 70s. His was wearing a makeshift sling that immobilized his right arm against his body. He was descending with a broken collarbone. He'd slipped on the initial downward slope from the summit. Ouch. Something to look forward to.

Still passing us were twelve-year-old girls and their semi-fit mothers. Whatever. It wasn't a race.

Eventually what Tim said became fact. It was the last slope up. We did get to the top. Yay. How did we do it? We kept going. We didn't stop. I hadn't stopped since that day long before when I said yes.

Funny thing about reaching the top of a mountain after a long, hard climb. The hike is only half done. Sure, it's all downhill from here. That's what the grandfather with the broken collarbone said. The hike down for him was much longer and more painful. The airlift was an option, but the cost reached into four figures, so he walked. We found out a park ranger connected with them and assured a safer descent. Good for them.

For me, going up meant looking up. Looking up doesn't bother people with vertigo and a fear of heights. I was also looking at my goal and not away from it. It means a lot when you're looking at your goal constantly. I couldn't see the peak, but I knew it was up. I kept looking up. I kept climbing up. Each step was one step closer to the top. I kept ascending. I was going to get **There**.

The Measure of Identifying Motives

Now I had to come down. Looking down. Heading down. A gravity-assisted-downward-momentum-kind of down. I was constantly looking out into the grand vistas that only the Rocky Mountains can give you. It was breathtaking. Gorgeous. Dizzying.

Down was part of the process. Down was part of the initial commitment in the first place. Too fast, and I was looking at a broken collarbone or maybe even a broken head. Ouch. There was no new goal or new commitment level here. What were my options? Stay on top? Nope. Call for a helicopter to pick me up? Just write a check. Down meant having to guarantee sure footing. Down meant controlling momentum. Down meant checking the gravitational pull on my body. It also meant very focused eyes. For someone with my elevation symptoms—fear and vertigo (I've mentioned it before three or four times)—I couldn't enjoy the vistas as much. I had to become singularly focused. The next step. The next handhold. The next boulder to shimmy over, around, or even under. Until I got back to the boulder field where walking didn't require leaning into cliff faces and clutching cracks and crevasses, I was seriously focused. It wasn't that bad, but in my mind it was.

To enjoy the views, I had to stop, secure myself, feel and embrace said security, and then, only then, look out to enjoy what God had created for us to soak in. I stopped a lot. Mostly to catch my breath and my nerves. It was harder for me to descend. Several things come into play.

First, the goal was already achieved. I had reached the top. Done. Accomplished. I was **There**. Coming down was the consequences of the achievement. Not quite as exciting. Rather anti-climactic. But it was part of the overall experience. The peak was realized. That's what I saw as the goal. The whole day should have been the goal with the peak enshrined as the highlight of the goal.

Second, did I mention the fear of heights and vertigo? Oh, yeah. Sorry. Part of the accomplishment of getting **There** required facing my fears. I had to do that. For me, it was not only the fear of heights. It was the fear of going beyond the boulder field, going through the Keyhole, and continuing with the unknown, hard, steep part of the climb.

Finally, the fear of success meant looking down and facing my fears in a whole new way. Too many of us are not as afraid of failing as we are afraid of succeeding. Why? We're afraid of success—what it might do to us and how it might change us. We get comfortable failing so that we don't have to face succeeding. Success scares more people than you can imagine.

Getting **There** required me to ask "Why?" several times. Why am I on the side of this cliff? Why am I putting out a tremendous amount of effort to get on top of a tall rock? The list goes on. Answering the Why question multiple times helped me up the mountains as well as down.

We made it down. More than fifteen miles over sixteen hours. Long day. Goal achieved. It was achieved before I set foot on the trail. Weeks before.

Getting **There** requires a bunch of Whys. More than one. As many as possible is good. Let's make a list.

Write your **There** at the top of a blank sheet of paper. Concise. Direct. Smart. Good.

Now, start writing every single reason known to mankind as to Why you should go **There**. Step away from the computer, use an actual piece of paper, and your favorite pen. Handmade bullet points of every reason to head **There**, starting today.

Frame it in the context of starting today. Doing this eliminates the idea of procrastination. If you're doing this right now, you are starting to head **There** right now. Identifying motives is a necessary part of the journey.

The Measure of Identifying Motives

Let's be very clear about what motives are. Motives are not feelings. Too many times people confuse motivation with feeling.

Mel Robbins, another author and motivational speaker, has this to say about motivation.

> *Forget motivation; it is a myth. I don't know when we all bought into the idea that in order to change you must "feel" eager or "feel" motivated to act. It's complete garbage. The moment it's time to assert yourself, you will not feel motivated. In fact, you won't feel like doing anything at all. If you want to improve your life, you'll need to get off your rear end and kick your own butt. In my world, I call that the power of a push.*[10]

So, motivation is a myth, but motives are something different. There is a difference. Let me explain.

- Motivation is short-term. "A sudden motivation to grab a 900 calorie, $5 caramel latte since I'm passing by a coffee shop."

- Motives are long-term. "Since my goal is losing weight and I gain by having too many carbs, I won't stop for that large caramel latte this morning."

- Motivation is manipulative. "Everybody wants me to try it, so I'm going to go for it." (Hold my beer.)

- Motives are rock solid. "Everybody wants me to do this but it doesn't get me any closer to where I ultimately want to be so saying no to the crowd is easy." (I'll hold my own beer, thank you.)

- Motivation is a fickle feeling. "I feel great this morning so I'll go for that 5K run." "I feel lousy this morning, so I'm gonna sleep in."

- Motives are anchors. "I feel lousy/great/whatever this morning, but to lose those last few pounds I will run my planned 5K."

- Motivation is measured in degrees or percentages. "I'm not very motivated today, but I'll give it a shot."

- Motives are 100%. "100% is easy. I've already made that decision, so I won't have to waste any energy deciding again."

- Motivation compels us to act impulsively. "Oooh, that looks cool. Let me try that."

- Motive compels us to act immutably. "If it deters me from getting **There**, I will not alter my course."

Motivation is different from Motive. I want you to list motives, rock solid reasons for you going **There**.

Still got that piece of paper? Good. Fill the page. Write down every single motive known to mankind you can think of for you to get **There**.

Rules. Yes, rules.

1. No reason is too trivial to list.

2. No reason is too dumb to list.

3. No reason is off limits to list.

4. Stop after twenty, unless you're on a roll.

Once you have this stellar list, walk away. Leave it face up on your desk, kitchen table, fridge, wherever. Leave it for one day. Not two days. Not a week. One day. Make an appointment in twenty-four hours to come back and grab that sheet of paper. Plug it into your handheld computer with the phone app attached. Set an alarm on your handheld computer with the clock app attached to use a loud, obnoxious siren to remind you in twenty-four hours.

Have a family? Smart spouse? Smart-alecky kids? If you do, you can try this:

> Leave the list face up on the kitchen table along with two colors of Post-It notes. Tell your family to read your nice, concise **There** statement, and all of your reasons why. Lay it out there.
>
> One color represents additional reasons to add to your own list. The other color represents reasons *not* to go **There**. Grow some tough skin and let them go at it. Funny, serious, inane, smart-alecky—collect them all. Nothing is off limits.

No family? Be bold and do this.

> Post your **There** on Facebook. Tag/invite your five best friends to give input/reasons. Make it private to them or not, your call. You'll get more than you asked for, I'm sure. In theory, in an open post, more than your tagged friends will want to toss in an opinion. Prepare for any/all replies. *Remember*, do not get discouraged by the negative. Feed off the positive. It is, after all, *your* **There** and no one else's.

Now, sit down with your list and hundreds of Post-It suggestions. Go through every one. Read them out loud, and immediately eliminate every one that goes against your overall purpose in this world. Rabbit-trails will turn a short walk into a marathon of detours and irrelevance.

Whittle down what's left to five or six solid reasons for you to go **There**. Now, choose one from this short list as your "absolute, never surrender, irrefutable, uncontestable" anchor motive.

Take the time to rewrite these motives in more precise and positive single sentences. I'd strongly suggest memorizing not only your **There** statement but also your motives as well.

Why? If **There** is important to you, memorizing it word for word reinforces its importance and your commitment to it. Memorizing your anchor motive is necessary when you're facing setbacks, early morning blahs, and unexpected deterrents. (Yes, there will be setbacks. We'll cover that in a later chapter.)

When going **There**

> When the daily grind is grinding deep into your heart
>
> When the world seems to be beating down your door
>
> When the weather sucks and the basement floods
>
> When you're tired
>
> When the masses laugh at you
>
> When your friends doubt you
>
> When the devil whispers in your ear
>
> When you're walking uphill, against the wind, in shag carpet
>
> When you feel all alone and see little progress
>
> When finish dates need to be altered, extended, adjusted
>
> When your daily habits get interrupted
>
> When your daily routines are suddenly derailed
>
> When you want to quit altogether

The Measure of Identifying Motives

Recite your **There** statement and your anchor motive.

"I am going **[There]**, and this is why [Anchor Motive]."

It wouldn't be a bad idea to make this a daily habit. Every morning, grab that laminated, framed, waterproof, encased **There** Statement and Anchor Motive and read them out loud. Read them both a few times every day in fact. You might think this is a bit over-the-top. So what. This is a great way to memorize and internalize these most important words. Consistent, spaced repetition. Boom.

Many people like to use visuals to remind them of their **There**.

Have you ever seen the movie, *Collateral*, starring Tom Cruise and Jamie Foxx? Foxx's character is a taxicab driver who carries a picture tucked in his cab's visor. It is a sailboat that he dreams of owning one day. He sees it every time he gets in his cab for a shift. Later on in the movie, the Cruise character challenges him with the fact that he's been driving a cab for many years and has never moved any closer to owning the boat of his dreams.

> *Someday? Someday my dream will come? One night you will wake up and discover it never happened. It's all turned around on you. It never will. Suddenly you are old. Didn't happen, and it never will, because you were never going to do it anyway. You'll push it into memory and then zone out in your Barcalounger, being hypnotized by daytime TV for the rest of your life. Don't you talk to me about murder. All it ever took was a down payment on a Lincoln town car. That girl, you can't even call that girl. What the **** are you still doing driving a cab?*[11]

It's only a dream; a **There** without legs.

Many people today create vision boards. To fully appreciate the phenomena that is vision boards, you must get into

Pinterest and search for vision boards. Thousands of visual examples will flood your screen. They're huge, small, detailed, vague, precise, wide-spread, artistic, crude, all-inclusive, all-of-the-above visions for their dreams.

I'm not talking about that. They are kind of cool to peruse, though.

What I'm talking about is a visual of one thing that will remind you of your single **There** and Why.

Some examples:

Climbing that volcano. (Here we go with the volcano again) Print a picture of that volcano. Boldly print the date of when you're going to climb it *on* the picture. Write your anchor Why on the back.

Losing 20 lbs. A picture of a slimmer you with this equation on it: [current weight – 20 lbs. = target weight] If you don't have a slimmer you, use a picture of a current you and draw your own curves on each side—) (—like that. It's a goal. Visualize it. Write your anchor Why on the back.

That beach. Again, print a picture of that beach. Write the time and date down of exactly when you will walk onto that beach. Write your anchor Why goes on the back.

That epic hike you want to do. Take a stone and put the start date of the hike on it. (Use a Sharpie!) Carry it in your pocket every day. Sadly, ladies, I wouldn't suggest using a purse. Things get lost in purses. I went into my wife's once. I got lost. I was thankful for good cellphone coverage and a GPS. You know what I mean. Wouldn't want you to lose your **There** visual in a black hole next to the lipstick you thought you lost three months ago. (I jest. Lighten up a bit.)

The Measure of Identifying Motives

Carry this tangible **There** with you everywhere. Laminate it if you take it into the shower or tub. Place it where it is the first thing you reach for every morning. (Unless you're married. Okay, when you get out of bed.) For me, that would be right under my glasses and on top of my phone.

Know your Why. Have as many other reasons as you need, but have one anchor motive. Since you have a goal to get **There** and you know Why, what could you do about it?

PART II: Get Your Rear in Gear

*Architects are not builders but overseers of the build.
You have to be both architect and builder.*
Bill McConnell

Everything up to this point has been book-learning.
Everything up to this point can be done on paper,
just like a blueprint from an architect.
Lists, thoughts written down, goals written, rewritten,
and motives defined.
It's been lovely, hasn't it?
Dreaming of leaving Here, going **There**.
Defining **There**, tweaking **There**, mapping out **There**.
I love planning. I love planning so much
I became certified as a Project Manager.
Serious planning there.

You may be a planner as well.
Everybody loves a flawless blueprint.
If so, you've loved this first part of the book.
At least, I hope you have.

Many times, people who love planning have a
hard time doing.

Conquer What's Next

Not all planners have this problem, but many.
I speak from experience.

This section isn't about planning. It's about doing.
It's about taking the lists and goals and habits and motives
you have drawn out of your Why
and putting legs and effort into them, to start going **There**.

Get your rear in gear and get at it. Goals are hard work.
Get at it. You've got this.

6

THE HUB OF DAILY HABITS

What will you do daily to get there?

Success isn't overnight. It's when every day you get a little better than the day before. It all adds up.
Dwayne Johnson

What can you do today that will get you one step closer to your goal? Consider these two questions as you transition from dreamer to doer.

*What **could** you do daily to get There?*
*What **will** you do daily to get there?*

Habits are **a conscious, daily activity you've chosen not to live without.**

That definition is different from most others you may have heard. For example,

Noun:
    a settled or regular tendency or practice, especially one that is hard to give up.
    a long, loose garment worn by a member of a religious order or congregation.

That's the definition when you ask Google for an opinion. There's very few of us who can pull off wearing a long, loose garment daily so let's stick with the first one. Here's a more detailed thought/definition of habit from an expert.

> *Every habit has three components.*
>
> *There's a cue, which is like a trigger for the behavior to start unfolding; a routine, which is the habit itself; the behavior, the automatic sort of doing what you do when you do a habit. And then at the end, there's a reward. And the reward is how our neurology learns to encode this pattern for the future.*
>
> Charles Duhigg

Now, Charles Duhigg is a very smart individual. It's safe to say that he knows what he's talking about. I don't doubt him for one minute. The science is there and which he explains it very well. Thanks, Charles.

James Clear, a blogger, speaker, and writer, whose focus is on habits and performance is another thought leader in this area. Here's his definition, from his own website:

> *Habits are the small decisions you make and actions you perform every day....*
>
> *What you repeatedly do (i.e. what you spend time thinking about and doing each day) ultimately forms the person you are, the things you believe, and the personality that you portray.*[12]

In your journey to **There**, every day you must take one more step. Let's face it. Some days you need to be reminded.

Okay, so remind yourself. As Duhigg suggests, set up some triggers, reminders of your goal, along with the methods you employ to get you there. You may have some behaviors in your life right now that will help you get **There**. You also may have some behaviors that will hinder you from getting **There**.

Reaching your goal needs to be behavior-driven, but it needs to be the right behaviors. Habits are these behaviors, and you can set up triggers to make you take these actions. Create new habits to get you through the daily grind.

Continuing with James Clear, he suggests setting a system in place instead of setting a goal. I agree, and I disagree. First, here's what James has to say:

What's the difference between goals and systems?

- *If you're a coach, your goal is to win a championship. Your system is what your team does at practice each day.*

- *If you're a writer, your goal is to write a book. Your system is the writing schedule that you follow each week.*

- *If you're a runner, your goal is to run a marathon. Your system is your training schedule for the month.*

- *If you're an entrepreneur, your goal is to build a million-dollar business. Your system is your sales and marketing process.*[13]

I agree because I see Clear's "systems" as a set of habits or a routine. I disagree because these "systems," or routines, need to be designed and put in place to support achievement of a goal. You need to define your **There** and know your Why. Then you will realize there's no way you'll reach that goal without developing a system that propels you toward that goal.

Now consider Leo Babauta's contribution to the idea of habits. He's taught courses on habits to thousands of people over the years. I couldn't find an actual definition that he uses when talking about habits. He does, however, discuss making small changes in your life to rid yourself of a bad habit and replace it with a good habit. His best article can be found here: https://zenhabits.net/36lessons/ It is worth the read, but later, not now.

Now I drop my definition into the mix.

> *Habits are a conscious, daily activity you've chosen not to live without.*

It is not contrary to the established definitions given above, except for the one about the long robes. It is my wording that I wish for you to embrace. I have a reason, a big reason, for you to do so. It is because I believe this and I will emphasize it for obvious reasons.

EVERYTHING REVOLVES AROUND YOUR DAILY HABITS. EVERYTHING. When you're concentrating on leaving Here so you can get **There**, you must be actively doing something to make that happen every single day. Your pursuit of realizing your goal revolves around your daily activities, activities you choose to do yourself.

To quote James Clear again:

> *Your life today is essentially the sum of your habits. How in shape or out of shape you are? A result of your habits. How happy or unhappy you are? A result of your habits. How successful or unsuccessful you are? A result of your habits.*[14]

If James Clear is correct, getting **There** will be the result of your habits. Stated another way, the result of your habits is achieving your goal. Also, staying Here is the result of your habits. What's to say you can't deliberately choose your own daily habits that propel you from Here to **There**?

Nothing. Nothing at all. That's what this chapter is going to focus on.

The Hub of Daily Habits

My definition one more time. You'll find out why in a few minutes.

> **Habits are a conscious, daily activity you've chosen not to live without.**

Break it down:

"conscious"

You are awake and aware. Getting from your Here to your **There** will take a conscious effort on your part. You can't sleepwalk through this journey, literally or figuratively.

"daily"

Every morning when you wake up, it's a new day. Like it or not, you get to start over. The good news is you don't start over from "Square 1." You start over from wherever you were the day before. You are making progress: incremental, consistent progress. This is not the Tom Cruise movie, *Edge of Tomorrow*, or Bill Murray's, *Groundhog Day*. You don't start all over again every day. You continue every day, and your daily habits are what will propel you from your Here to your **There**.

"activity"

You are doing something. You are active in your own movement from Here to your future **There**. You actively exercise. You actively say no to too many carbs. You actively get up early every morning with purpose. You actively read your "**There** Statement" to reinforce where you are headed. You actively "_____."

"you have chosen"

    Remind yourself that this is your choice. This is not the choice of your spouse, your boss, your neighbor, the critical masses, the negative Facebook commenters, or Twitter trolls. This journey is yours. You have chosen to go boldly toward your goal, so you have also chosen to do daily whatever it takes to get you **There**.

"not to live without"

    How long can you hold your breath? For me, not that long. I like breathing. It is an unconscious habit that keeps me alive. Your daily habits that you choose to do every single day needs to become something you refuse to live without. Think of it as the breathing that keeps your goal alive so you can get **There**.

This idea of habits as a daily decision needs to be directly connected to your achievement, your purpose, your goal.

Consider the following question very carefully.

What could you do daily to get there?

Make a list. Yes, another list. At the top of a piece of paper, write down once again your articulate, well-thought-out goal. It never hurts to write out your goal. It solidifies it in your mind, and you will do whatever it takes to achieve it, to get from Here to **There**.

Make a list of activities you can put into your life daily to reach your goal.

Here's an example:

My goal: I will to lose thirteen pounds and weigh no more than 162 pounds by December 1, 2017.

Here's what I could do daily to reach that goal:

- Weigh myself every morning at the same time.

- Walk two miles every morning before 8:00 a.m.

The Hub of Daily Habits

- Say no every day to foods that I know will not help me lose weight.

- Hmmm ... Let me try that last one again ...

Say no every day to foods that have too many carbs in them. These foods are _____.
(Be as specific as possible without losing your mind doing so.)

- Work out every morning using an app on my iPhone called "7-Minute Workout."

- _____

The actions on this list are part of the routine, or set of habits, that I have currently designed to meet this goal. The goal is mine. I will get there. It is not a huge goal, nor is it a challenging goal. I need to lose some weight.

Now, please realize the wording of the question. Here it is again.

What could *you do daily to get there?*

What *could* you do? Not what *will* you do. That comes in the next chapter. Right now, it's what *could* you do. It's a list. Make it an exhaustive list of as many crazy daily ideas as come to mind.

Tune in to your goal, your end result, your eventual achievement, and brainstorm every single daily activity, no matter how minute or outrageous it may be.

- Count every calorie (MyFitnessPal app does this)

- Count every carb (MyFitnessPal app does this as well)

- Count every bite (Why?)
- Record every rep (Just a little OCD)
- Record every step (Fitbit or iWatch or something else)
- Record every mile (Map My Walk app on your smartphone, or Fitbit, iWatch, etc.)
- Record every weigh-in to the tenth of a pound.

(MyFitnessPal app is amazing. It does this too.)

- Create a chart so you can daily see your loss of weight. (Yup, MyFitnessPal app can do this)
- Cut off another inch of my right leg beginning at the toes – that should be about thirteen pounds by December 1. (Maybe not that one, it would make the rest much more difficult)

The key here is the idea of a daily activity. Daily. Seven days a week.

You want to lose weight: Exercise daily.

You want to run a 10K: Train daily.

You want to get that promotion at work: Visualize daily (among other things).

You want to write a book: Write 1,000 words daily.

You want to know God more: Read the Bible daily.

You want to vacation in Europe: Save money daily.

You want that new car: Spend less daily, and save daily.

You want less stress in your life: Meditate daily.

The Hub of Daily Habits

You want to be smarter: Read daily.

You want to get **There** from Here: _____

_____ : _____
_____ : _____
_____ : _____
_____ : _____
_____ : _____

I'm sure by now you get the idea. So, make a list, keeping focused on the idea of *daily*.

I understand that to achieve your goal, it will take some planning and effort that goes beyond making a list of things every day. There will be milestones along the way, and many other things that are not daily activities.

As an example, your trip to Europe does not require you to buy a ticket every day until you go. Nor does it mean you pack something every day until you go. (To be honest, though, I believe my wife does pack something new every day for the whole two weeks prior to any trip we take. It's her way of doing it.) What I am strongly suggesting is that every day you do something that gets you closer to reaching your goal, that gets you from Here to **There**.

> *An important component of having a goal tied to a habit is that it allows you to size your habit proportionally to the goal. If you want to lose weight to look better, maybe you need to lose one pound per month for a year. That will allow you to create an easily sustainable habit that will get you to your goal and still leave you plenty of capacity for other habits or obligations on your time and willpower . . .*[15]
>
> From the book *Superhuman By Habit*
> by Tynan, blogger and world traveler

Everything revolves around habits. What could you do daily to achieve something amazing in your life?

Make another list. A long, insane list of every single idiotic thing you could do daily to get you closer to your goal. Make it a habit-listing marathon. Nothing, and I mean nothing, is too stupid to put on the list.

Let's try it.

You want to *become a morning person*. So, every day, in no particular order:

- Set your alarm for 5:00 a.m.

- Set your alarm on the other side of the room when you go to bed.

- Before going to bed, fill a glass with water, and put a quarter lemon wedge in it.

- Prep the coffee maker the night before. Does it have an automatic start timer on it? Set it for 5:01 a.m.

- Get out of bed when the alarm goes off.

- Use a tangible, visual reminder of your #1 motive for becoming a morning person. Put it on top of whatever you reach for when you wake up.

- Go to bed no later than 10:00 p.m. the night before.

- When you turn the alarm off, head away from the bed.

- Turn everything off by a certain time every night.

- Set tomorrow's clothes/housecoat/sweats out every night before getting to bed.

- Every night, inform your spouse or significant other, of the time your alarm will be going off.

The Hub of Daily Habits

- Know where you're going when you get up. Go there.
- Know what you're going to do when you get up. Do it.
- Drink the lemon water you prepared the night before.
- Have a cup of coffee.
- Exercise. Move.
- Take a walk. Take the dog for a walk.
- Read. Have the book waiting for you when you get up.
- Meditate. How long? Where? How?
- Pray.
- _____
- _____
- _____
- _____
- _____

You see where we're going with this. Consider the possibilities. All the possibilities. Every single possibility. Put every possible daily action or activity that you could do on the list.

This is everything you could do, but it's not everything you will do. Overload can kill a goal quicker than anything else. It's the theory of "Gung Ho." Gung Ho sends you off in the general direction of your goal, but you may be doing too much. You've settled on a goal and want to go after it with full force. Full force, however, may get you to quit. Unless you take some time to fine-tune your Why and consider everything you could do, you end up doing too much. Too much can kill your momentum. It's not sustainable.

With this huge list of what you could do, let's get realistic and consider what you will do.

> *A good plan violently executed now is better than a perfect plan executed next week.*
> General George Patton

Since *habits are a conscious, daily activity you've chosen not to live without*, what are you willing to commit to do every day?

Let me put it another way.

What **will** *you do daily to get There?*

You have a list of habits you thought you could do every day. Habits you've defined as beneficial to getting you **There**.

So, you know your overarching why, you've determined your **There**, anchored down your motives, and thoroughly exhausted your possible daily actions to get you **There**. So, what? Nice stack of papers, eh? It doesn't have to be. It shouldn't be, and I'll tell you why. You already know this, but I'll remind you anyway.

Your Why, your purpose in life, and your Goal are worth the effort. Getting **There** is worth your time, your pain, your schedule adjustments, your money, and your daily grind. It is a testament that you are not going through life at the whim of whatever blows your way. No. You are choosing to live forward. Living today with a future before you.

My wife works one day per week as a Nurse Practitioner in the clinic at our local university. She has many stories to tell. It's easy work for her because 95% of the time all she deals with are strains, sprains, and STDs. The other 5% are flu-like symptoms. Many times, she educates these young adults (particularly the freshmen) that there are long-term consequences to short-sighted decisions. Most of them have yet to discover their Why. If they knew it, they would be much less likely to be in her clinic.

They have no compass, no defined purpose, and no vision of what's ahead for them. Committing to daily habits has little value to them because they are not connected to a greater sense of purpose. They have no idea what **There** is to them.

Hopefully, that is *not* you.

Change Your Normal

Normal is comfortable, expected, and easy. You've created your own normal. Let's remember that normal is a relative term. Normal for Michael Phelps while training for a swimming competition is sheer lunacy for you and me. So, let's forgo comparing our normal with someone else's normal. It isn't fair to you or the other person.

When considering the habits, you want to incorporate into your day in order to get **There**, remember the following:

- Your normal is nobody else's. Don't compare.
- Your normal must change, or you will not progress.
- Gradual change ensures lasting change.
- Consistent change ensures progress.

In Daniel 6, we read of a habit that put Daniel in a very dangerous position.

> ¹⁰*Now when Daniel learned that the decree had been published, he went home to his upstairs room where the windows opened toward Jerusalem. Three times a day he got down on his knees and prayed, giving thanks to his God, just as he had done before.* NIV

Just to keep things in perspective, in this passage Daniel is a captive of the Persian empire. He is a prisoner, a slave, who was fortunate enough to be placed in a position of leadership. He lived in one of three places to oversee 120 satraps, also slaves. Cream rises to the top. Daniel was the cream.

Darius, king of Persia and the Medes, was convinced to *"issue an edict and enforce the decree that anyone who prays to any god or human being during the next thirty days, except to you, Your Majesty, shall be thrown into the lions' den."* Daniel 6:7 (NIV). The next thirty days was all about worshipping King Darius. Not for Daniel though. Daniel resolved to keep his own habit, a habit of praying three times a day to God, not Darius.

Daniel did what he had always done. It was his habit. It was his resolve. It was his commitment to God. Word of Daniel's daily habit reached the king.

Darius did not want Daniel to die. He liked Daniel. Nevertheless, a law is a law, and Daniel was tossed into the lion's den.

Daniel's daily habit got him arrested. Daniel's daily habit earned him the death penalty. Daniel's daily habit had him live out his faith in the presence of big, hungry felines.

Daniel purposed what he would do daily regardless of the situation or circumstances.

What's the point of a good habit if you're not going to keep it every day?

Am I suggesting that your habits are so firm that they simply don't flex or bend at all?

The Hub of Daily Habits

Consider bamboo versus plastic.

I am kind of a rigid guy—mostly black and white. When I get handed an acronym for a morning ritual, I want to do those tasks in order every morning. I feel like I'm failing if I don't. I wrestle with making adjustments.

The danger with this wrestling is that if I lose, I want to give up. I am not bamboo. I am hard plastic. This is not a good thing.

Back in 1995, I went to Hong Kong to visit my sister. It was her third year living there, and no one from the family had gone over to see her. Since my mother was seventy-seven years old at the time, and I'm the only sibling, I won. Yay for me. I love to travel.

I'd never been to Asia, but I'd seen pictures. I couldn't wait.

Once there, many things seemed so foreign, such as how the locals did things and how they lived. Nothing wrong with that, just different.

Once in the city itself, the biggest difference I noticed was not the building methods or the structures. It was the scaffolding. In America, OSHA-approved steel rods bolted together reach up against the side of buildings for both new construction and maintenance. The scaffolding in Hong Kong city was not like the scaffolding in America. In Hong Kong, it was primarily made from bamboo. It was amazing.

The bamboo used as the scaffolding takes about four years to grow. It is then cut into lengths of seven meters and tied together with a variety of materials.

We're not talking about two-story houses here. We're talking about high-rise buildings, in the heart of the city, hundreds of meters into the air. Bamboo is very strong and very flexible. These are the two key elements to the most durable natural wood on the planet.

At no time in my travels, to Hong Kong or anywhere else in the world (I've been to twelve countries), have I ever seen hard plastic scaffolding. Never. Can you believe it? I'm sure you know why. Plastic breaks. Can you imagine trying to convince workers to build scaffolding with plastic rods instead of bamboo? These guys' lives depend on the strength of this scaffolding. What would their answer be? "Nope."

One year, on the day after Christmas, a father had to deal with his seven-year-old who had broken his new favorite toy. The boy cried and cried. Dad's response was typical dad-speak, "It is plastic, and it will break." That phrase stuck with the kid from that day on. Plastic breaks.

Plastic is not all bad. If it doesn't have to hold the weight of a guy hundreds of meters in the air, then plastic is the thing to use. Each has its own uses. A bamboo car bumper or a set of bamboo Tupperware doesn't make sense. Plastic scaffolding doesn't make sense either.

We were discussing morning rituals earlier, weren't we? So what's with the plastic and bamboo rabbit trail? It's more about rituals. What works better for you? A plastic morning or a bamboo morning?

Plastic Habits: Flexible, almost to a fault, or hard and brittle. In either case, not very strong.

Bamboo Habits: Flexible to a point, and naturally very strong. It only comes one way, and that's okay.

In the world of great analogies and comparisons, plastic and bamboo may not make the top ten. Plastic isn't as bad as it may seem, and bamboo isn't perfect. However, when it comes to creating meaningful habits in your life, lean more toward bamboo, and stay away from plastic.

A routine, especially a morning ritual, has to be flexible to accommodate changing schedules and situations. There also needs to be a point where you say you will keep that morning ritual no matter what. The best routine is flexible to a point, then strong with resolve. This works best when you have designed the routine so that the habits within it are natural to you and your personality.

Leaving what you could do for what you will do.

Take that list of all the things you could do and get realistic about it. Lose the ones that you know won't happen. Focus on the few that will get you started. Remember, you're heading toward achieving something new and amazing in your life. How practical and doable are each of these habits? Be honest with yourself. Which ones could you put into practice tomorrow? Which ones could you start to do today?

For each habit you add to your day, determine a trigger, a reminder, for that habit.

- If your goal is to lose weight, and your habit is daily exercise, what will trigger your memory to start this activity?

- If your goal is getting a Master's Degree, congratulations. What daily habit will get you closer to that degree? How will you remind yourself daily to do that?

- If you have a lifestyle goal of better hygiene, yay. Your habits are brushing, flossing, and showering every day. What are the triggers to get you to do that daily?

- If your goal is to climb a mountain and your habit is daily exercise ... wait ... exercise again. Sounds more like a lifestyle habit than an end-game goal.

You get the idea. Choose habits that you will do. Make them part of your everyday life. Be flexible on the timing, but don't compromise on the doing. Don't fit them into your current life. Place them in your life and adjust the rest of your life to make sure they are kept.

Set up a "Seinfeld Calendar" to accomplish this. This simple idea is explained in the next chapter. You have to start somewhere. Decide what habits to start with and start. We're past the planning stages now. Get at it.

7

THE REVEALING OF ROUTINES

How will your habits work together?

The key to developing a deep work habit is to move beyond good intentions and add routines and rituals to your working life designed to minimize the amount of your limited willpower necessary to transition into and maintain a state of unbroken concentration.
Cal Newport, "Deep Work"

A "routine" is a string of habits, and a "ritual" is a habit charged with transcendent meaning.
Gretchen Rubin, "Better Than Before"

Routines have a bad reputation. That's kind of a bummer. Never mistake a routine for a rut. Ruts are bad. Routines don't have to be. Routines can be the key to getting you through the rough part of the journey as you head **There**.

Ruts won't get you **There**. The key to getting out of a rut is to actively invest yourself in passions that resonate with you.

How will your efforts work together?

Steven Pressfield, author of *The War of Art*, makes no bones about it. He blames our social ills, anxiety, and drug-dependent tendencies on our habit of giving in to the resistance (the voice that tells us we can't do things), and not doing the work that matters to us. Perhaps we would do best by acknowledging those things we know we love.

I see habits and routines as very close friends. I believe routines are made up of a strategic set of habits. Each habit can stand alone all by itself. Exercise . . . all by itself, every day. Shower . . . all by itself, every day. Hydrate . . . all by itself, every day. Get up early . . . all by yourself, every day. All are habits in and of themselves. None needs the other to exist and be effective. But this is a routine: Get up early, hydrate, exercise, then shower. That's a pretty good morning routine. Not only that, but they work together to help each other be even more effective.

Order is also important. You don't shower, then exercise. You don't hydrate, then decide to get out of bed. The right habits grouped together into a routine creates synergy. They work together for a greater overall effect. You set a trigger for the first habit in the routine, then each successive habit triggers the next.

To have a purpose and a goal to fulfill is one of your greatest assets. Give your day-to-day struggle a sense of meaning, effort, and reward. You would do well to spend your time creating things that satisfy you fully, move you toward your goal, and honor a higher purpose.

Chaining habits. . . . Moving through your chain, even once it becomes routine and ordinary, is very satisfying. You know that it will accomplish the major requirements of your day, yet it becomes so automatic that it feels effortless. It's through this process that habits give you freedom – chains take care of the necessities of life, and leave you with time and willpower to make forward progress.[16]

The "Seinfeld Strategy"

Brad Isaac was a young comedian starting out on the comedy circuit. One fateful night, he found himself in a club where Jerry Seinfeld was performing. In an interview on Lifehacker, Isaac shared what happened when he caught Seinfeld backstage and asked if he had "any tips for a young comic."

Here's how Isaac described the interaction with Seinfeld:

He said the way to be a better comic was to create better jokes and the way to create better jokes was to write every day.

He told me to get a big wall calendar that has a whole year on one page and hang it on a prominent wall. The next step was to get a big red magic marker. He said for each day that I do my task of writing, I get to put a big red X over that day.

"After a few days, you'll have a chain. Just keep at it and the chain will grow longer every day. You'll like seeing that chain, especially when you get a few weeks under your belt. Your only job is to not break the chain."[17]

James Clear has this to say about the Seinfeld story:

You'll notice that Seinfeld didn't say a single thing about results.

It didn't matter if he was motivated or not. It didn't matter if he was writing great jokes or not. It didn't matter if what he was working on would ever make it into a show. All that mattered was "not breaking the chain."

And that's one of the simple secrets behind Seinfeld's remarkable productivity and consistency. For years, the comedian simply focused on "not breaking the chain.[18]

I've used the Seinfeld Calendar to break a few bad habits. One, which I will not mention, has had a hold on me for too many years. I started a chain on January first. I never broke this chain, not for a single day. The red X for this bad habit became an obsession for me. I stopped using the chain after about five months and continued beating the habit into non-existence in my own life. The mental red X over each day was a win for me.

I've used this method for not watching TV before 5:00 p.m. It's four feet away from me, in my home office. We have cable, Netflix, and even Amazon Prime. (Don't ask) On top of that, I love watching a good movie. Sadly, I even like watching bad movies simply to watch a movie. The struggle is real. TV can be such a time-sucking, useless activity. I admit to losing a day, here and there, and the chain is broken. We're all human, right? The goal is never ever let it go beyond one day. Start a new chain and resolve to go longer than the last chain. Longer and longer stretches of unbroken chains.

I've used the concept for work as well. I write down three things that must be done the next day. I label them my OTTs. The initials come from the book *Organize Tomorrow Today* by Jason Selk and Tom Bartow. The discipline is to write down three main tasks you will do tomorrow, then do them. It has done wonders for my productivity and for not wasting time. I have three things to do every day, even on days I don't do work. Mowing the lawn creeps in there every Friday. I hate yard work of any kind, but I do mow the lawn.

Maya Angelou woke up at 5:30 a.m. *every morning. She would drink coffee with her husband around 6:00* a.m., and at 6:30 a.m. when her husband went to work, she would too. She went to a hotel room that she kept for writing. She would arrive at 7:00 a.m., and work until 12:30 p.m. or later depending on her creative flow. Her routine helped her become an amazing and inspiring author.

The Revealing of Routines

Sara of unsettle.org has this to add to the positive side of routines.

Routine is boring. We use the word "routine" as an indicator of dullness. Of the opposite of excellence. And that's a shame. Because routine works. Routine sets apart successful people from the unwashed masses.

And why does it work so well? Well...

Routine removes decision fatigue: *... Think of your mind like a gas tank. With each decision you make, you use more fuel. So if you use all of that decision power deciding what to do when you wake up, what to eat, and how to structure your day, the decision-making fuel you have left for the important decisions you must make is nil.*

Routine ignites creativity: *Have you ever wondered why you have the best ideas when you're showering, driving, or just before you fall asleep? What do those things have in common that spark creativity? Well, you don't have to think about them. They're routine. They allow your mind to wander. They allow you to daydream.*

Routine makes you more successful in everything you do: *Part of my routine is to wake up every morning and write 1,000 words before breakfast. Writing is an important part of my online career – in fact, it hinges on writing. So every morning that I write 1,000 words before breakfast, that's a small win. I've made progress. And humans are far more motivated by progress than by anything else. When I've made progress through my routine in the form of a small win, I'm going to be more successful in everything that I do throughout a day. I'll be more inspired to carry that through to other aspects of my work and my life.*

Routine helps you move forward: *If you build productive work into your routine, your routine will help you achieve your objectives – even if you don't feel like doing the work. If my routine is to wake up every morning and write 1,000* *words before breakfast, then I do it. Because it's my routine. Even when I don't feel like writing, it's my routine to write, so it gets done. Think about it—you probably have a routine to brush your teeth before bed. Even if you don't feel like doing it, you brush your teeth before bed. It's just part of your routine.*[19]

That was a lengthy quote, but it was worth it. Continue to think of routines as a set of habits chosen to keep you moving closer to your goal every day.

Some people quietly stand out over time. This is due in part to the fact that they've been involved in their chosen field for a long time. As a starting pitcher, Nolan Ryan's career spanned twenty-seven years with four different teams.

I know we've covered this. However, Nolan Ryan is the all-time greatest pitcher, with seven no-hitters, three more than any other pitcher. He's tied with Bob Feller for the most one-hitters, with twelve, and has eighteen two-hitters. As I related before, he did it by committing to a workout schedule, and never deviating from it.

The question I have is, "Did Nolan Ryan start his career with a detailed, daily exercise routine already in place, or did he develop it over time to become as good as possible for as long as possible?"

Somewhere early in his career, he realized that to be the best he could be for as long as possible, he'd need a daily routine that would keep him in the best shape possible for his particular position. Looking back, here's what he had to say about it:

"A lot of people were amazed to see me on an exercise bicycle immediately after a game, while my arm was being iced . . . I did it to cleanse my muscles of lactic acid and get an aerobic benefit that pitching can't give me, and to stay on course with my training."[20]

Take another look at your chosen habits. You know, those habits that you *will* do, habits you know you *have* to do, to achieve going **There**. They can work together. You have to find your routines and rhythms in life, like riding an exercise bike while icing your arm.

The Synergy of Cooperating Habits

The best way for me to describe synergy is this: I can load a truck with 100-pound bags in an hour by myself. I lift them up onto the tailgate, then climb up, pick them up again, and stack them. But if you help me, and you can also lift 100 pounds, we can load that truck in twenty minutes with one of us on the ground, and one in the truck. We have created synergy. When you begin to get into a daily rhythm of working toward your next achievement, begin asking the question, "How will my habits work better together?"

Constantly tweak your daily activities to help create synergy.

Now come the monkey wrenches—the breaks, the unexpected, the unannounced visitor, or the broken thumb. It seems as soon as you find yourself making slow but methodical progress with your habits and routines to get you **There**, the monkey wrench gets thrown at you.

Just remember this one thing:

> *If you can dodge a wrench, you can dodge a ball.*
> Patches O'Houlihan,
> in the movie *Dodgeball*

8

THE ADMISSION FOR NEEDED ADJUSTMENTS

How well will you adjust to change?

> *Remember the 5 Ds of dodgeball:*
> *Dodge, duck, dip, dive and . . . dodge.*
> *Dodgeball*, the movie

The dock on the lake in the evening was gorgeous. I loved youth camp. So much energy. So much fun. So many high schoolers goofing off. So many opportunities for teaching moments.

This youth camp had its own lake and a boat dock as well. For some reason, I found myself on the dock, alone. As I turned to head up the hill, I was met by four high schoolers. Gotta love them. I'd known them for several years. Great guys. They wanted to have some fun with the Camp Director—me.

"You're getting wet." It wasn't a question. It was a statement.

"Really? How so?" I immediately replied. You have to be quick with teenagers. Give them too much time to think, and they may formulate a plan.

"We're throwing you in the lake." There's four of them and one of me. Seems logical. So I agreed with them.

"Okay. I'm going in the lake. I have one question before this happens." Like I said, you have to stay ahead of these guys. Sure, they had a plan. Four teenagers throwing one adult in a lake. Great fun. That was their only plan. I, however, had a plan of my own.

"What's the question?" They were mildly curious.

"Which one is going with me? I'm not getting wet alone. I need to know which one wants to get wet with me."

Clearly, I was banking on the idea that none of them wanted to get wet themselves. Luckily, I was right. They could have grabbed me, and all of us could have gotten wet together. Great times, right? That wasn't part of their plan. Their plan was to get me wet while all of them stayed dry and safe on the sturdy dock.

They looked at each other and surmised that there was no way on earth any of them were getting wet. There's four of them. There's only one of me. Seriously, how were any of them getting wet with me? I love it when egos jump in and make people believe themselves unbeatable. Over-confidence is great!

They rushed me. I went low and braced for impact. They didn't want to hurt me. They wanted me to get wet. I didn't want to get hurt or get wet. So there we were. Four against one wrestling on the dock and I had the advantage.

Yes, you read that right. I had the advantage. More than one. Let me lay it out for you.

They didn't want to hurt me. Cool. They would show a certain level of restraint.

They didn't want to get hurt. Also cool. Restraint.

None of them wanted to get wet. I didn't care whether I got wet or not, but I wasn't going to concede.

I had already conceded in my own mind that I was getting wet. No big deal to me one way or the other. I had nothing to lose. Having nothing to lose was a big advantage.

Back to the docks. Every time they felt they had me in a position to toss me in the water, I had a serious grip on one of them. Remember my plan. I wasn't getting wet alone, and they knew it. As a matter of fact, I made sure they knew it. I kept asking them the entire time which one wanted to go swimming with me. By doing this, the one in my grip stopped the other three from tossing me because he didn't want to get wet. I chose my anchor, and the anchor told the other three, "Wait a minute, let up, get a different grip" whatever. It was awesome.

Funny thing about loyalty. These guys stuck together and respected the wishes of the group. Why not toss Bill *and* one of them in the lake? Mission accomplished, right? Not really. Their plan, deeply ingrained in their heads, was that I was getting wet and they weren't. Deviating from the plan was not an option for them. Their group loyalty provided another advantage for me.

This went on for several minutes. They had me in different positions, but I always had a grip on at least one of them. If one of the others tried to break the grip, I'd let go and latch on to that person. I was having a blast. I was also getting tired. Tired and sweaty. North Carolina has high humidity.

Getting tired was a disadvantage for me. I had to end this quickly. You may not like this, but I was committed. I was more committed than any of them. In the fray of bodies all over the dock, the hairy leg of the supposed ringleader ended up in my face. Yes, his calf, to be exact. What's a guy to do? I bit him. No blood. Nothing so serious. I bit him enough for him to realize I was more serious than he was.

Immediately, he pulled away from the pile screaming, "He bit me." He was right. I did bite him. He didn't realize my alternate plan. He thought I was going to get wet. I even told him I was going to get wet, along with one of them. What I didn't tell them was that I wouldn't give up trying to stay dry.

Within a minute, the others quit as well. Fear of the next bite? Maybe. However, they were tired as well. Enough was enough. I never got wet. Neither did any of them. No one was watching, so no egos were damaged in the process. There was talk about it later. I still wonder what their rendition was. I wonder if I left a scar on Randy's leg. I doubt it. I'll have to ask him.

So, how did I come out on top when the odds were four to one against me?

- Assess your opponents' parameters. I knew the commitment level of the other four.
- Know your own parameters. How far will you go?
- Make sure your parameters go further than theirs. The further yours go beyond theirs may do more than level the playing field. It may even give you an advantage.
- Have a plan they don't expect. Have a plan that messes with their expectations. Their plan: Bill got wet. They stayed dry. My plan: Bill and one of them got wet.

All of this deals with making adjustments.

- Enjoy the sunset. Four teens wanted me wet. Adjust.
- Devise a plan of defense. Adjust.
- Four teens tackled me on the dock. Grab one. Adjust.
- They had an advantage. Grab someone else. Adjust.
- Getting tired. Bite someone. Adjust.

The Admission for Needed Adjustments

Wrestling one or wrestling four, it didn't matter. Wrestling was a constant state of adjusting to your opponent's adjusting.

I achieved my moment of **There**—enjoying a sunset on the dock. However, it was short lived. If I wanted to stay **There**, I had to make some serious adjustments quickly.

Another movie that I absolutely love is *The Martian* with Matt Damon. The last five minutes of the movie are worth the price of admission *and* the loan taken out to buy that popcorn/medium drink combo. I do suggest that you watch the whole movie to get the full impact of the last five minutes. I'm not spoiling anything by giving you this last monologue. If anything, I'm giving you a reason to watch the whole movie.

> At some point, everything's gonna go south on you ... everything's going to go south and you're going to say, this is it. This is how I end. *Now you can either accept that, or you can get to work. That's all it is. You just begin. You do the math. You solve one problem ... and you solve the next one ... and then the next. And If you solve enough problems, you get to come home.* All right, questions?[21]

The italicized section is for emphasis. Too many people in life have already accepted "ending." It may be years before they die, but they've ended. They've stopped solving problems. Everything went south, and they let it. They've accepted defeat years before they had to.

We were driving to Indianapolis. Yay. Our youth group was all pumped up for this one-week urban mission trip. We'd come off an amazing national rally, and now we were ready to change the world. Yeah, that's how we thought back then. Nothing wrong with it. Off we went.

For a few of these kids, this was their first time out of the state. Seriously. Big adventures for them. The van atmosphere was crazy. That mood lasted forever. We left early, leaving crying mommas in the parking lot. Prayers for safety and "journeying mercies," all that stuff.

I'm a planner. I love to lay out the details, cross the "t's," and stuff like that. The route was simple enough. Head northwest from home, which at the time was Asheboro, NC, on I-74, which turns into I-77 in the southwestern point of Virginia. A quick jaunt west on I-81 before veering north on I-77.

We never left I-77. It joined I-81 for a few miles. It was all interstate. They all looked the same. Two, three, or four lanes headed in both directions. On-ramps, off-ramps, some traffic. You know. All the same. This trip was before the days of personal GPS devices and cell phone apps. It was the days of paper maps and AAA Trip-Planner flip folders. The only verbal cues came from the shotgun seat.

The shotgun seat was very important. Almost as important as the driver. Being shotgun meant navigating well and being a second set of eyes for the driver. Shotgun also had to keep the driver awake and supplied with Krispy Kreme donuts. Sugar and coffee were essentials on trips like this.

When we hit the North Carolina/Virginia border, we all screamed and yelled, acknowledging to our "never-been-out-of-the-state-before" kids that they had, in fact, left the state. "*Virginia!* You're in Virginia. Welcome to world travel. Join the club. Your parents are hours behind you and can't do a thing about it. Yay." On we went.

Did I mention we left at three in the morning? Still dark when we took off. Still dark when we hit the Virginia line. The state line celebration was spontaneous, but I knew we had to keep it up. It was fun, energetic. It kept us awake. Every little milestone was celebrated, keeping everybody engaged whether they wanted to sleep or not.

Interstate blended into interstate, and as time and miles went on, the early morning caught up with us. Energy waned. A few kids started to sleep. I was driving because, as the

The Admission for Needed Adjustments

fearless leader, I had to be in control. Before you knew it, another state line came up on us. I started it off once again. "Hey, we're in Tennessee." Everyone screamed again. Another milestone accomplished. Another state conquered by our border breach. The energy picked up again.

Then I stopped cheering. Everyone else was fine. I stopped. Why did I stop the elation? What was wrong? The van was running fine. We still had a few donuts left. The weather was great. So what?

"What are we doing in Tennessee?" It hit me first because I was the planner. I was the route maker. I was the leader. What were we doing in the great state of Tennessee? The interstates all looked the same. On-ramps, off-ramps, some traffic. You know. All the same.

I looked at our shotgun occupant, a little glaze on the lower lip and a bit on the chin. "What are we doing in Tennessee?"

"Aren't we supposed to be in Tennessee? You're driving. You tell us what's wrong."

Oh, it was like that, was it? The driver blamed the navigator. The navigator blamed the driver. Back and forth we went. Hey, it was both our faults. It was nobody's fault. It was the weather's fault. Not really. It was great driving weather. Wait ... It was the Virginia State Department of Transportations' fault. Poor signage. That was it. Poor signage.

Now, since many of you aren't intimately familiar with the area being described, we should never have been in Tennessee. That short jaunt where I-77 and I-81 share asphalt for about six miles was only for about six miles. I-77 takes a ramp to the right and heads north. That's the ramp we wanted. That's the ramp we missed. That's the ramp that was about an hour behind us now. Oops.

Stopped on the side of the road, before too much time passed, we had to make some decisions. Same route or reroute? Backtrack or adjust? Interstate or cross-country? Four-lane familiarity or two-lanes into the unknown? You already know where I'm headed with this. Where's that map?

Let's head north. How bad could it be, seriously?

The original route was to be North Carolina, Virginia, West Virginia, Ohio, and finally Indiana. But we were in Tennessee. So now it became North Carolina, Virginia, Tennessee, Kentucky, Ohio, and Indiana.

I needed to keep the crew together on this. The whole trip was an adventure all by itself. Now we would see something other than interstate. Interstates are great for A-B travel. We were doing that. We only had one day scheduled for the A-B part of this trip. At the end of the day we needed to be in Indianapolis. I felt it important to get the team back to our original route.

When we discovered the variation to our route, a few of the younger ones did freak out. In youth ministry, everything that happens is an opportunity for a life lesson, a spiritual lesson, or a lesson of some other kind. No matter what happened, it was going to be a lesson. These kids were going to learn something, even if what they learned was that the driver missed the ramp. I was determined to keep a positive spin on everything.

Positive Spin #1. Those first-time travelers got to claim not one but two extra states in their travel journals. As a person who's been to all but four states in his lifetime, I call this a positive spin for these young travelers.

Positive Spin #2. We would see something other than an interstate. Give me some scenery, please. Interstates are not the best for great vistas and inspiring lookouts. At least, not in this part of the country. It's mostly trees and divided highway, with the occasional massive truck stop strategically placed along the way. Now we would see small towns and true Americana. That's how I sold it.

The Admission for Needed Adjustments

Positive Spin #3. The general-store-with-the-candy-counter option.

Now, when adjusting in the middle of a project, there's a tendency to want to veer back to your original track. It is familiar. You spent time planning, and you want to get back to that plan. You're comfortable with that plan. You liked that plan. That plan would have worked, if not for the missed ramp.

Sometimes adjustments to the unplanned can open doors to new possibilities. Possibilities you never would have discovered by sticking to the original plan. The incident opens the door to a new route, a better route, a more efficient route.

That was not the case for us. We needed to get back to the original route. Efficiency while driving great distances does involve extensive use of our interstate system. Our adjustment needed to get us back on the interstate we missed way back there. Out came the paper maps.

"If we head this way, the road doesn't look that bad." No one can tell what the road was like by looking on a paper map printed several years ago. However, it did get us going in the right direction again. That was the point. We quickly agreed on a plan and got the van moving again.

We couldn't afford to waste more time. Quick decisions had to be made. We'd already lost time and distance by missing the ramp. I've mentioned missing the ramp several times because, well, I was driving, and missed the ramp. We missed the planned route. We missed the right turn. We were off course, and it was my fault. After all these years, I am taking ownership of my poor eyesight and inability to read road signs early in the morning.

I know how I missed the ramp, by the way. There are several reasons.

Reason #1. Inattentiveness. I wasn't watching. (I blame the co-pilot. Shotgun seat has responsibilities.)

Reason #2. Too comfortable. You know how even when you're driving, you get in a comfortable groove while going down the road.

Reason #3. Temporary lack of focus. Just for a few minutes, at the wrong time, I forgot the next turn. It totally left my mind. I knew we had to get off I-81 a few miles after we got on I-77. I knew that. I planned the trip. I planned the route. I briefly forgot my own plan at the wrong time.

All of these reasons blend together and feed off of one another. Inattentive, unfocused, comfortable.

The off-route adjustment became somewhat of a nightmare for some. The back roads weren't as good as how they looked on the map. No shock there. One of our girls sitting in the back threw up. There are more hills and turns when not on an interstate. Pros and cons there. The scenery was better, but we ran out of Krispy Kreme. I don't remember a single small town that captured our interest. Probably because our focus was getting back on route. Not on that general-store-with-the-candy-counter we all wanted to visit but couldn't because we needed to get back on route. Need I say more?

We adjusted. We kept going. We got back on track, and we did make it all in one day. Sure the day was a few hours longer. We had better stories when we got back home. After the fact, it was a blast, except for the throwing up part.

The easy choice would have been to backtrack on the interstate and get on with the trip. The most functional choice would have been to backtrack on the interstate and get on with the trip. The better use of time would have been to backtrack on the interstate and get on with the trip. We chose adjustment.

Adjustment opens doors. Doors you never saw before. Doors you would have missed completely had it not been for missing that ramp.

The Admission for Needed Adjustments

Adjustment forces creativity. We could head this way or that way to get back on track. Which one is better? Maybe it doesn't matter. Get creative and get back on the road.

Adjustment forces redirection, which the very nature of adjusting. The direction must still get you to your original goal. Sometimes the best redirect is to turn around, find the ramp you missed, and get on with it. Sometimes it's major adjustments. Either way, it's an unplanned redirect. Live with it. Own it. Get on with it.

Adjustment gets you back on track. You don't change your overall goal based on making adjustments. We still needed to get to Indianapolis. We didn't head to or stop in Lexington, Kentucky. It wasn't an option because it wasn't our overall goal.

Would we take that adjusted route the next time we planned that trip? Are you kidding? Nope. The next time, the driver won't miss the ramp. As a matter of fact, he'd be so intent on getting it right, the kids would have to be quiet, the radio would be turned off so he could see better, and total laser-like focus would dominate those few miles. You adjust when necessary. You don't do it for fun.

How was the trip home? Spot on. Never missed a turn. Never veered off course once. Fully focused and intentional in every aspect of the drive. We didn't want Diana hurling in the back seat again. We didn't want to run out of Krispy Kreme. We were also tired. The end of a trip is so much different than the front end. The energy is different. The expectations are different. Adjustments at the end are so much harder to take. We got home safely with stories to tell about the trip and not about the last day on the interstate.

With the end in sight, a straight route becomes a very high priority. Interstates provide a lot of straight routes. Nobody thought about the general-store-with-the-candy-counter. Well, maybe one or two of us thought about it, but we didn't want to stop there. We wanted to get home. Other adventures awaited us.

Monkey wrenches should never be a problem while in route from Here to **There**. Expecting them is the best thing you can do on your journey. There is no straight path, no easy, level road anywhere, except maybe in Kansas and parts of Nebraska.

Adjustments are part of life. We constantly adjust to stay on track. There's a totally unverified story from years ago when cruise control first became available on small motor homes. Some guy bought a brand-new motor home, with all the bells and whistles, including cruise control. You guessed it. First time out on the road, he sets the cruise and then slips into the back to grab a cola (or a beer). Crash, bang, holiday over. Hope he had insurance because the warranty doesn't cover stupid.

Driving down a straight road in Kansas, or any state, takes small steering adjustments to go, well, straight. And by straight, I mean between the lines. My wife insists on this, by the way. This is important to note: No steering adjustments are needed when the car is standing still. None whatsoever.

When having making adjustments to your journey, the first thing you need to know is where you are. Get a point of reference before deciding the next step.

> "What is the best way to eat an elephant?" Answer: "One bite at a time." Lanny Bassham, an Olympic gold medal shooter calls this handy precept the "ready, fire, aim" principle. Lanny claims that in sports and in life, people spend too much time aiming at the bull's-eye and not enough time shooting at it. Rather than placing so much emphasis on getting ready and aiming, go ahead and take a shot. Taking the shot gets you started and also lets you gauge how far off the mark you are. Make adjustments, but keep

The Admission for Needed Adjustments

shooting until you get closer and closer, and eventually you will hit the bull's eye."

Jason Selk, *Ten-Minute Toughness*[22]

Some adjustments are huge, like discovering you're in Tennessee when you should be headed to Indianapolis. Other adjustments are small. Two inches to the left of bullseye. Make a minor adjustment. No big deal. The result is the same as long as you keep driving or keep shooting.

Now think of an airplane. They have more than cruise control. They have, wait for it, autopilot.

Autopilots adjust course constantly, to correct for the wind. This is a good thing. Here are some interesting stats about flying one-degree off course:

- For every degree you fly off course, you will miss your target by ninety-two feet for every mile that you fly.

- For every sixty miles you fly, you will miss your target by one mile.

- Flying around the equator will land you almost 500 miles off target.

- Flying from JFK to LAX will put you nearly fifty miles off course.

As you head from Here to **There**, small adjustments may have to be made. Don't sweat it. Make the adjustment when you realize one needs to be made. Your goal is still within reach. Getting **There** is still very possible. Don't wait. The longer you wait, the more off course you may find yourself.

While we're at it, you've heard the inspirational phrase, "Aim for the moon. Even if you miss it, you'll find yourself among the stars." This is a terrible idea and not at all inspiring. NASA wanted to go to the moon. What if NASA said, back in 1969, "Hey, we'll get you close. It should work if we did the math right. We're good at math. In case we're off a bit, you'll be among the stars. Good luck." The first words out of Neil Armstrong's mouth were, "Nope. I'm out." (I paraphrase.)

Going to the moon was NASA's goal. They wanted to go **There**. They made adjustment after adjustment after adjustment. Spoiler alert: They landed on the moon. Neil, Buzz, and Michael did not slip off into the void of space. The sun is our closest star, and all that would do is make things very hot. "Among the stars" is a terrible place to end up.

Getting to the top of Volcán Pacaya is very different from the trek to the top of Volcán Acatenango. Yes, I've been on top of both. One was a morning stroll and, well, you already know about the other one. That climb was worth doing. Stick to your goal, and plan to make whatever adjustments are necessary to get you there. Be like NASA, not like a tourist in Central America who has fulfilled a bucket list goal by not being picky.

The Adjustment Plan

There is no adjustment plan. You need to plan to adjust.

There was a procedure I used when planning youth camps and retreats. It was a simple walk-through. I would mentally walk through each aspect or phase of the event.

- The tech guy will be here thirty minutes beforehand to set up. Who's doing that? What if he can't make it? Who's his backup? Is there a backup to the backup? Is there an emergency plan B?

The Admission for Needed Adjustments

- The food. What about the food? Who's bringing what? Who's in charge? Who's their backup?
- We need ten youth leaders for this event? What if we only have seven? How will we adjust the number of teens to the leadership?

You get the idea. Walk through your own process of getting from Here to **There**. Make mental plans to adjust when things get off course. Don't panic. Adjust. Plan for the flat tire. Plan for the unexpected expense. Plan to reschedule if necessary. Contingency plans are great when you need them, and a source of relief when you don't.

PART III: Gain the Grit to Go There

Our potential is one thing. What we do with it is quite another.
Angela Duckworth, author of *Grit*

Angela developed a written test that measures the predictability of which candidates who would drop out of Beast, a seven-week training program for incoming freshmen at West Point.

You are challenged in a variety of ways in every developmental area – mentally, physically, militarily, and socially. The system will find your weaknesses, but that's the point – West Point toughens you.
West Point Cadet who survived Beast.

Grit has to do with two things in a person's life:
Perseverance and passion.
Not SAT scores, physical ability, leadership ability, IQ.

To answer the next three questions, consider your own perseverance and passion when it comes to you getting **There**.

9
THE RESILIENCE OF RESOLVE

How desperate are you to succeed?

Many people think that what the addict needs is willpower, but nothing could be further from the truth.
Arnold M. Washton, Ph.D.

If you want to make any permanent change in your life, willpower won't get you there.
James Clear

Willpower is for people who are still uncertain about what they want to do.
Helia

Once you make a decision, the universe conspires to make it happen.
Ralph Waldo Emerson

When your desires are strong enough, you will appear to possess superhuman powers to achieve.
Napoleon Hill

Conquer What's Next

If your why is strong enough you will figure out how!
Bill Walsh

If you're required to use willpower:
- You haven't made up your mind.
- Your desire (your why) for your goals isn't strong enough.
- You haven't fully committed to what you're going to do.
- Your environment opposes your goals. Thus, you haven't created an environment that makes your goals inevitable.
Willpower sucks. Forget about it.

James Clear

Wow, that a lot of quotes. Which one did you like?

Let me get this straight. You're telling me that willpower sucks and yet, you have a whole chapter devoted to it as the last link in the process. Hmmm. No. This is a chapter about Resolve. The quotes were about willpower.

Resolve is different from Willpower. Much different.

Okay, let me explain. Wait. Let the dictionary explain first.

will·pow·er
ˈwilˌpou(ə)r/

noun

1. control exerted to do something or restrain impulses.
"most of our bad habits are due to laziness or lack of willpower"

re·solve
rəˈzälv/

noun

1. firm determination to do something.
"she received information that strengthened her resolve"

THE RESILIENCE OF RESOLVE

Von Miller Goes to Hell and Back[23]

There are thirty-two NFL football teams and each one of them is preparing for a serious run at playing in the Super Bowl. Yes, all thirty-two of them. Even Cleveland. For the record, I'm a Bronco's fan.

At the end of the 2016 season, outside linebacker and Super Bowl 50 MVP, Von Miller, fell one vote short of being the NFL defensive player of the year. He also happened to fall two and a half sacks short of the league lead, and his Broncos fell one victory short of a postseason berth. Von was not a happy guy.

Four days after the final regular season game, Von Miller decided to go to hell and back.

"Hell's Trainer" lives in San Francisco and is lesser known by the name Frank Matrisciano. He has no website, no twitter account, no Facebook page. He wears a hoodie and sunglasses. He doesn't advertise. He is a private trainer. For every ten guys who start his training regimen, only three finish.

Miller rented a house in San Francisco, and every day that he could for about eight weeks, he endured Matrisciano's "Chameleon Training," a grueling regimen that emphasizes adaptation to unstable environments.

Von Miller showed up at the Broncos' OTAs (Organized Team Activities) in better shape than ever before. Stronger, more explosive, and sending a serious message to his teammates that he wants to have a great season.

During OTAs, Miller flew Matrisciano to Colorado for "Chameleon Training" twice a week between team practices. Afterward, they returned to California for additional weeks of work before Miller reported to Training Camp.

I think Von Miller is serious about reaching some new goals he has for his career. He's not yet done achieving personal goals in his life.

Now, I'm writing this after the fifth day of 2017 training camp. Only time will tell if Miller has become the super-athlete he wants to be. He's not realized any of his goals yet. He may. He may not. That's all in the future. But Von Miller is serious about his goals, his career, his team, and his teammates.

Every day Von Miller is thinking about and working toward goals and standards he's set for his life. Every day Von Miller does something to carry him a little closer to his goals. Every day he's serious about it.

Every day.

Pyambu Tuul represented Mongolia in the marathon at Barcelona in 1992. He came in last. When asked why he was so slow, he replied, "No, my time was not slow, after all you could call my run a Mongolian Olympic marathon record." Not satisfied, another reporter asked him whether it was the greatest day of his life. To which came the reply, which would throw anybody off their seats. "And as for it being the greatest day of my life, no it isn't," he said. "Up until six months ago, I had no sight at all. I was a totally blind person. When I trained, it was only with the aid of friends who ran with me. But a group of doctors came to my country last year to do humanitarian medical work. One doctor looked at my eyes and asked me questions. I told him I had been unable to see since childhood. He said, 'But I can fix your sight with a simple operation.' So he did the operation on me. After twenty years I could see again. So today wasn't the greatest day of my life. The best day was when I got my sight back, and I saw my wife and two daughters for the first time. And they are beautiful."[24]

It's the races that we run within ourselves that are most important.

I feel it's important to note that in that race twenty-five runners quit. Tuul was so slow, the race officials rerouted him to an alternate finish line so they could set up the stadium for the final ceremonies. But he finished.

And then there's the story of John Stephen Akhwari, a Tanzanian Olympian who struggled to complete the 1968 Olympic marathon after he fell during the race cutting and dislocating his knee. He refused help from any officials and chose to continue the race. He pushed himself through the pain and one hour after the race had already been won, John Stephen Akhwari finished the race. When asked by a reporter why he didn't quit he replied, "My country did not send me 5,000 miles to Mexico City to start the race. They sent me 5,000 miles to finish the race."

I could add a third example of Derrick Redmond[25] running the 400 meter in the London Olympics. Look that one up yourself. The video is inspiring.

Now, let me ask you this question as the last step of the process of achieving a great life accomplishment, which is you getting **There**.

How desperate are you to succeed?

When Bear Grills, or some other wilderness survivalist TV show, gets desperate for fluid, they suggest drinking your own urine. Now that's desperate. That's the point.

Resolve is reminding yourself every day that you've already decided to go **There**.

- You've already decided to exercise this morning. All you must do is exercise.

- You've already decided not to eat that bagel for breakfast. All you must do is not eat it.

- You've already decided to stick to a morning routine. All you must do is complete the morning routine.

- You've already decided to write 1,000 words every day until your book is complete. All you must do is write 1,000 words.

- You've already decided how to adjust when the unexpected happens. All you must do is adjust and keep going.

- You've already decided to do whatever was necessary to get you **There**. Now all you must do is get **There**.

I find it interesting that, as little as five years ago, willpower was touted as the necessary ingredient in the process of achieving anything. Willpower implies something that requires us to work. Work hard at something. There's nothing wrong with working hard. We'll never get anywhere without doing it. Willpower is "willing yourself" to do those last few repetitions in the gym, "willing yourself" to run that last 100 meters to the finish line, "willing yourself" to say no to the cinnamon roll next to the register at the coffee shop.

Resolve goes beyond what willpower gives you.

Imagine this: Two of "you" are standing in line at the coffee shop to get, well, coffee. Both love a little sugar rush every now and then. I know I do. Both see the enticing allure of a fresh cinnamon roll with frosting, ready for a quick zap in the microwave. The person in front of you turns and walks by your nose with that very same cinnamon roll freshly zapped for the consumer's pleasure. Yum, right?

Both of you order your coffee. The first "you" struggles, eyes on one of the last two rolls on the counter. Just this one time. It'll be okay. You've been good for weeks now. You hesitate, your mind struggling to decide to buy or not to buy. It's painful, but finally, you decide to roll with coffee. You turn and walk away from the counter a victor—a winner, a non-cinnamon-roll-eater. You stared the enemy in the

The Resilience of Resolve

frosting and walked away without any sticky fingers whatsoever. Congratulations. Willpower!

The other "you" steps to the same counter. Same coffee order, same two cinnamon rolls, same frosting, same subtle aroma, same zap-able option. You've been good for months now. Same everything, except hesitation. No hesitation. No struggle. No pain. No decision to make. You order your coffee and leave. No internal expending of emotional energy. As you leave, you whisper to yourself, "That was easy."

Why was that so easy? Resolve. Why was it hard for the first "you" who struggled, hesitated, took a second whiff, and pined inside? Why was it so easy for the second "you" and not the first "you"? Why? Resolve. The decision had already been made.

I was in Phoenix, in April 2016, at a Launch Conference held by Jeff Walker. I learned a ton about internet marketing and getting projects off the ground. This was the phrase, the one statement, that stuck with me above everything else.

The resolve of the second "you" kicked in because you were 100% committed to getting **There**. Not 99%, but 100%. Once you realized and internalized that **"100% is easy. 99% is hard."** you were 100% committed to the process and priority of getting from Here to **There**, little things didn't throw you off your game, or your path.

If your **There** is to lose twenty pounds in three months, ignoring one cinnamon roll is easily ignored. The time and energy of daily exercise or a three-mile jog is easy because you want to get **There** and nothing is going to stop you. Why? **"100% is easy. 99% is hard."**

You already said no to the cinnamon roll before you knew it was even there. Before the frosting, the aroma, and the zap-warming option. No was the answer before you got out of bed that morning. There's no need to answer a second time. Why is that?

Answering a second time implies you're still at 99%. But you're not at 99%. You're at 100%. The difference of 1% is the difference between struggle and ease, hesitating or doing.

You may be thinking: both walked away without the cinnamon roll. Both won. Yes, both. All experts will tell you that willpower is like a muscle. Muscles get tired. Muscles need rest. Muscles can fail. Too many pushups, and eventually you will stop. The first "you" muscled your way past the sweets. The second "you" had no struggle because there was nothing to decide. The decision had already been made.

Experts also tell you that your willpower is stronger in the morning than later in the day. Why? Because you've been using your willpower throughout the day on many little decisions and it's now tired. A good reason not to make decisions at the end of the day. Especially big ones. You're tired. You want to rest. You're more susceptible to breaking a diet in the evening than in the morning.

Back in my freshman college years, a group of us headed to a nearby city to go swimming in the Olympic-sized facility at another university. Hey, I can swim, so let's get wet, right?

Well, this was my first time *ever* seeing a facility of Olympic specifications—an accurate way to describe it. You'll find out soon enough. I came from a very small town, and I didn't get out much. Swimming I could do. Water is water. However, everything changed when the group decided to take on the ten-meter tower. I'd never been on a ten-meter tower before. How bad could it be?

Bear in mind, I have been wearing glasses since the age five and am quite nearsighted. I don't swim with my glasses. Therefore, everything was out of focus and fuzzy. Here we go.

Bowing under the pressure of my peers, as well as the ladies all watching us do our jumps, I got in line to, well, jump. There was a line, and I was in it. When I got to the first ladder which went up to the three-meter board area, there was a sign I read when I got close enough. Holding onto the ladder, and before my first step up, I read it.

**No one is allowed to come down the ladder.
If you go up, you must enter the pool
from the platform.**

Something like that. You get the idea. Up I went.

Please understand, at this point in the process, the sign says if I go up, then I'm committed to diving or jumping. Either one. Don't believe that for one second. The sign has nothing to do with my personal commitment to getting wet from great heights.

There was a lifeguard or two that kept things in order. No goofing off. No pushing or shoving, or stuff that would get someone hurt. They also gave the nod for whoever was next to climb the ladder. So, there I was, with the lifeguard's permission, climbing to the three-meter platform. Guess what I found? A three-meter diving board, of course. I also found another ladder and another sign. The sign said the same thing as the first sign. No shock there. They're cheaper when you buy in volume.

Bypassing the diving board option, because we all said we were going off the ten-meter tower, I approached the second ladder and read the second sign. At the nod of the lifeguard (I'm assuming he nodded as I couldn't see him at all without my glasses) I headed up to the ten-meter platform.

In the online world, a platform is your brand and marketing that you build. Your products, teaching, blog, podcast, whatever you share with others is part of your platform. I found myself on a different platform, and it wasn't fun at all.

This was a physical platform of height and perceived prominence. Why the prominence? Well, only one person at a time could stand on it. Everyone who stands on it isn't allowed to use the ladder anymore. That's what the sign said anyway. Everyone up there can be seen by everyone in the pool area, and across the city, or so I thought. It was, of course, an indoor facility. Canada in the winter, so that was a given.

Please understand, at this point in the process, the sign says if I go up, then I'm committed to diving or jumping. Either one. Don't believe that for one second. The sign has nothing to do with my personal commitment to getting wet from great heights.

You've read that paragraph before, but it bears repeating. Two signs, two ladders, two paragraphs for emphasis.

Here I was standing alone on a platform ten-meters above the pool. I was all alone with everyone watching me. (I am certain that had nothing to do with my Speedo bathing suit. I don't know. It was the '70s.) Included in those watching were the lifeguards, charged with keeping everybody safe and sticking to the rules of the posted signage. So, in their minds, descending the ladder was not an option. Not to them. It was still an option for me.

On that ten-meter tower for the first time in my life, I experienced a fear of heights. Probably because I knew I had to jump off the platform. I began to panic but caught myself. Why? People were watching. My peers were watching. The girls were watching. The lifeguards were watching. Everybody was watching. Everybody was watching me. It was my turn.

With a deep breath, I launched off that tower, executing for the first time a 2 ½ gainer with a full twist, and nailed the entry with minimal splash, something the judges look for. As I came out of the water, seven of the ten judges gave me 9's or 9.5's. Impressive, don't you think?

Okay, that didn't happen. I walked to the edge and looked down. What do you think I saw? Water? Nope. I saw nothing. I'm mostly blind, remember. I could not distinguish where the air stopped, and the water began. I had no perception of height or distance whatsoever. And the lifeguard said, "It's your turn. Jump."

Please understand that at this point in the process, the sign said if I go up, then I was committed to diving or jumping. Either one. There were two signs that said that. Don't believe that for one second. I say again: The signs have nothing to do with my personal commitment to getting wet from great heights.

To mask my fear and try to come out of this with some dignity, I did the only thing I knew. I started to goof off. Masking fear with humor has been around for centuries, and I was perfecting the process from the tallest "stage" in the area. I backed up and ran to the edge, stopping short, and smiling at the crowd. I think I tried to wink at one of the girls at that point, but who knows? I couldn't see a thing. I wasn't deaf by any means. I could hear friends yelling to make it a good one. I could hear the lifeguard say again, "It's your turn. Jump." This time, he said it emphatically.

Was I committed? Nope. If fear took over, the signs meant nothing. The lifeguard meant nothing. The slippery ladder that only goes up will go down. If fear took over, I would not get wet from great heights that day. Guaranteed. I was not committed until I decided to jump or not jump.

This time, fear did not win. Once again, fear was covered up. I backed up, took another comic run to the edge, and stopped again. I smiled again. I winked again. This ticked off the lifeguard again, who said one last time with complete seriousness for the position and the signage, "*Jump.*"

Was I committed? Once again, nope. Signs? Who cared? Lifeguard? Get a real job. Friends? I could get new ones. Girls? It'd be tough, but I could travel to distant lands and find someone in a remote village who hadn't heard of the platform guy who used the ladder instead of jumping. My fear was not the height. It was the fear of landing.

Everything bad ran through my mind. If someone drained the pool, I'd never know. I couldn't see. Were there people in the way? Maybe I should wait until it's clear. Maybe the lifeguard was wrong about the rules. Maybe the signs were a joke left over from last April. What if I broke a leg or an arm? What if I hit my head? The list was endless.

By the way, any excuse is a good excuse if you don't want to do something. You should see my list of excuses for not mowing the lawn each week.

Someone once said, "It's not the fall that kills a person. It's stopping at the bottom that does it." With one last goofy run for the edge, I carried myself a little too far based on the previous two times. On the third run, my momentum caused the central point of my body mass to pass beyond the edge of the platform. It was at this point I was finally committed (my unintentional 100%). I couldn't stop, so away I went. The ladders were no longer in play. The lifeguard stopped yelling, *"Jump."* I think he started yelling something else, but I wasn't sure.

I was committed. I could not turn back. I could not turn around. How would I be remembered? What would they write on my tombstone? I was committed. Do or die. I was heading over the edge one way or another. I was committed. On that platform, I left all of my doubts, excuses, whining, signage, impressing my peers, winking, the dream of 2 ½ gainers with a twist, masks of humor to cover it all up, and yelling lifeguards. I went fully committed headlong into the great unknown.

Well, unknown to me. Sure, I knew the water was still there. It was silly to think otherwise, but you do think of things like that when you're afraid to commit to something. Especially something that scares the bejeebers out of you.

I know you're dying to find out how it ends, right? Did I stick the entry? What were the judges real scores? (Hint: There weren't any judges and there was no competition.)

The Resilience of Resolve

I remember only one thing during my long-anticipated descent: Where's the water? It didn't take long to find it, experience it, inhale it (oops). Due to my inability to focus and straining to see the approaching water, I'm told I kept leaning forward to get a better perspective on my position. That's a nice way of putting it. I'm told the lifeguards took careful notice of me after entry to see if I was injured or even unconscious. I'm told that the angle of entry, which was barely feet-first, was well past 45-degrees. My jump was fast approaching belly-flop status. I kept looking for the water instead of trusting that the water was there.

And that is true commitment. You know it's there, but you can't see it. You have a hard time focusing on the tangible. You are filled with fear at times. You hide your true feelings way too much. You come up with the lamest of excuses for not stepping out, but you do anyway.

You even risk appearing the fool to lifeguards, friends, and girls you want to impress, but you do it anyway. None of those people matter. It doesn't matter to them if you backed out, and it doesn't matter to them if you commit to the jump.

It only matters when you let yourself down. Why? Because you let fear win. Fear got the better of you. Fear caused you to go down the ladder. Fear made you get out of the line. Fear kept you out of the water. Don't let fear win.

Now the analysts among us will think about my experience and say:

"So, you didn't truly commit yourself. You had a little too much momentum and slipped when you got to the edge." Nope. Try again.

"You were forced over the edge by lifeguards with loud voices." (Loud buzzer) uh uh.

"You did it to be included as one of the few, the brave, the ten-meter platformers." Hmmm. Initially, but not ultimately.

"You did it to impress the ladies." Seriously, after all that, there are better ways to impress the ladies. Did I mention I was wearing a Speedo? It was the '70s. Everybody was wearing a Speedo.

It wasn't pretty. It wasn't without flaws. It was rather embarrassing. It bordered on personal injury. It received all the wrong attention for all the wrong reasons. But I did it. I jumped.

You can view all the outside influences as either warnings or encouragement.

- Did the signs warn me of danger, or prod me to move forward?
- Was the lifeguard getting mad at me, or ensuring my personal safety throughout the process?
- Were my friends encouraging me to die at the bottom of an empty pool, or encouraging my opportunity to conquer a personal fear?
- Were the ladies going to applaud my efforts and all get in line to date me because they knew I could take fear and turn it into an accomplishment, or laugh at me for the rest of my college life?

(Okay this last one was a stretch, but I had to keep the theme going. You understand.)

Looking back, it's easy to see all of this. In the moment? Not so much.

In the moment, I could have filled my swimsuit with . . . well, you know. It was, for me, scary up there. In the moment, I was willing to move forward with what I had started. In the moment, I had every excuse possible to stop the process, but I didn't. In the moment, the signage, the lifeguard, my peers, the ladies, my reputation, everything, didn't matter that much. In the moment, all I had to do was jump. In the moment, I jumped.

The Resilience of Resolve

Note: There were some among our group who never got in line and never jumped. Why? Perhaps they already knew their limitations, they knew their fears, or it was no big deal to them to even try. At the time, I possessed none of those traits. They refused to push beyond their own boundaries, or they refused to face their fears. Either way, I jumped, and they didn't. They weren't embarrassed. They weren't yelled at by lifeguards. They didn't show any fear, and they didn't take any risks. They didn't go home with their chest hurting due to impact. Yeah, mine hurt. They had no story to tell about themselves. They only had my story to tell, and mine was one to remember. I jumped.

Jumping off is what you have to do if you want to reach a goal in your life. There is no reason on earth for setting a goal if you're not willing to go over the edge to reach it. Nobody sets their sights on middle management. They end up there. Nobody sets a goal of climbing half a mountain or half a volcano.

Okay, that's not completely accurate. I have on my bucket list the goal of making it to base camp on Mt. Everest. I view base camp as a final destination.

I had no resolve, no commitment, when I said I'd jump off that ten-meter tower. I decided to do it only to fit in. The struggle began almost immediately, and I had to decide again and again until I went off that platform. The exertion, the stress, the hesitation, the doubts, all forced me to use my willpower to get me up the ladders and over the edge.

Some of those who went up the ladders and past the signs, jumped when the lifeguards said the landing area was clear. They were either much quicker to make all the same decisions I made (unlikely), or they had resolved to jump before they ever stepped on the first rung. Resolve would have eliminated all those little crisis points.

Resolve reduces stress. Resolve focuses any exertion where you need it the most. Resolve has very little hesitation.

Resolve answers the doubts encountered along the way. Resolve exudes confidence, which is much more impressive than cheesy comedy to cover fear. And speaking of fear, resolve faces fear head-on and moves forward regardless.

Resolve Versus Willpower

Willpower is a decision to be made every time.
Resolve is a decision made once and kept.

Willpower gets tired as time wears on, like a muscle.
Resolve doesn't get tired because the decision has already been made.

Willpower is never more than 99%. There's still doubt that needs to be answered.
Resolve is 100%. There's still doubt, but it's already been answered.

Willpower is the same decision made many times.
Resolve is one decision made one time.

Willpower leaves the door ajar.
Resolve latches and locks the door.

Will Powers is a great stage name for a fitness coach.
Resolve is a great brand name for a carpet cleaner.

Willpower is control exerted to do something or restrain impulse.
Resolve is a firm decision on a single course of action.

Marriage is all about resolve. Love, of course, but resolve throughout a life of marriage. If you have the desire to read my first book, **TOGETHER,** it is about how my wife almost left me in our seventh year of marriage. She wasn't happy, but I was too blind to see it. When we got married, I committed—resolved—to never get divorced. It was not an option for me. When my wife opened my eyes to that possibility, I simply wouldn't have it.

Had I put my foot down and told her that would never happen, she would have been out the door quicker than free Krispy Kreme donuts at the church coffee bar, or Kentucky Fried Chicken at a church potluck. You get the idea. But I had resolved to never get divorced, so I did what few men learn early in their marriage. I shut up and listened. I listened and learned. Get the book. It'll be worth your time.

Resolve will get you up in the morning. Resolve will get you moving forward every day. Resolve will keep the hub of habits intact. Resolve is Matt Damon in the movie *The Martian*, saying, "I'm not going to die here." Resolve is winning before the start of the game. Resolve is you getting **There** before setting in motion your first habit and routine. Resolve is one step at a time, one day at a time, one habit at a time. Resolve is not quitting, it is adjusting and continuing.

Three Questions About Your Resolve to Getting There

1. What will it take to get you to settle for less?

2. What will it take to get you to change your mind?

3. What will it take to get you to quit?

All three answers are the same. If they're not, I question your resolve to getting **there**.
Your answer needs to be "*Nothing.*"
There's nothing that will get you to settle.
There's nothing that will get you to change your mind.
There's nothing that will get you to quit.
Nothing.

10

THE STOCKPILE OF SUPPORT

Who is going to help you get there?

Friends may come, and friends may go, but enemies accumulate.
Anonymous

How could she have done things differently? What other options would have created a different outcome?

In the 2016 Olympics, I watched the Women's Cycling road race. That's right. And I was on the edge of my seat for the last half hour.

Let me set it up for you.

There was a lead group of two riders, followed by a chase group of three riders. There was one long downhill stretch with steep grades, sharp turns, and it was starting to sprinkle enough to make the road wet.

There was an unlikely American racer, Mara Abbott, in the lead group, but in second place to the Dutch racer Annemiek Van Vleuten. Downhill was not Abbott's strength. Her strength was climbing, which is what got her to second place.

Van Vleuten was extending the gap between her and everyone else. She had it made. She was the gold medalist, as long as she kept two wheels on the road. But this was a race. Racers race. She raced.

One day earlier, the men raced on the same course. There were four in the lead group, and there was a crash among them. Broken bones. None of them finished or medaled. They were in the lead. They all ended up in the hospital. Every woman racing had that on their mind while descending the last hill.

Abbott played it safe. She raced within her skill set. She stayed steady. She was in second place all alone. She could feel a medal around her neck. A silver medal.

Out of nowhere, Van Vleuten miscalculated a turn. I guess that's what happened. All I saw was the crash. She went over the handlebars and landed on her head. She was out cold. In a split second, her race was done.

Thirty seconds later, Abbott went by, and everything in her mind changed. Now she felt a gold medal around her neck. Just finish. Stay strong.

Enter the chase group—another Dutch rider, Vans Der Bregge; a Swede, Johannsen; and an Italian, Londo Borghini. Three racers from different countries who knew that the only way to catch Abbott was to work together.

In cycling, the lone rider out front always has the disadvantage. They're constantly fighting the air resistance. In a group of two or more riders working together, they take turns fighting the air resistance. One is out front, and the two behind can pedal a little easier and stay right there.

In this case, three racers from three different countries cooperated to minimize the effects of the resistance. By doing so, they went faster together.

Abbott ran a great race, but her lead wasn't enough. She had spent most of her energy to put her in the position out front. Out front all alone.

Out front all alone fighting the air.

Out front all alone and quickly running out of energy.

The Stockpile of Support

Out front all alone within 200 meters of the finish line and a potential gold medal.

Out front all alone and passed by three people working together.

Abbott came in fourth place. No medal. No podium. No Olympic glory.

Ironically, the race was won by the teammate of the Dutch racer who had the lead and fell.

Abbott was not expected to medal. Other Americans on the team were better overall. Abbott happened to be considered the best climber in the world at the time. Climbing was what got her into a position to win.

How could Abbott have won?

Abbott could have won if the race was 200 meters shorter. She had no control over that. The race was set before anyone started.

Abbott could have won if her lead at the bottom of the hill was ten seconds better than it was.

Abbot could have won if one of her teammates had been there to help her. They couldn't keep up with her on the climbs. Abbott was the best in the world in climbing.

Consider this: Abbott beat the pre-race favorites. She beat her teammates. She exceeded her expectations. Sixty-eight competed. One was disqualified. Fourteen riders, who started the race, didn't even finish the race.

Here's what she had to say after the race.

> "I didn't believe it. I saw the 300 meters to go sign, and I thought 'holy s***, I can actually win this.'" Abbott said. "Then I looked under my shoulder, and they were right there, and they passed me. There was a split second when I thought it and then.... It feels awful, but at the same time, you were supported by a team that worked so hard and did so well to give you a chance to win. In some ways, I'm so disappointed to have not been able to give

something back, but in other ways, I'm one of the luckiest people in the world to have those people behind me."[26]

She credits her teammates for keeping her in the race and supporting her. Class.

Three riders won medals at the 2016 Rio Olympics because they chose to work together. They cooperated for a few miles to beat the resistance.

Never fight the resistance alone.

Who are your unlikely teammates that will get you through this day?

Who are you willing to work with this week that will help both of you get ahead?

There is something missing. Something important. Something that's not in the graphic, or listed as a chapter head. Without it you might still succeed. You might still get **There**. Congratulations. Without it, the chances of face-planting with the world watching (or maybe only your immediate family) is greatly increased. This missing link may be the difference between success and face-plant failure.

This link is other people and their encouragement. Not the encouragement you get from your morning mantra, or your "vision board." I'd love to make fun of vision boards right here, but they do have their place in many people's lives. They do help, and they are an encouragement. But here's the point. So far, it's all you and no one else.

You may need outside encouragement, help, support, love, prodding, and so on from—gasp—other people.

There, I said it. Other people.

You know what that means, don't you? You're going to have to let other people in on where you're going. You're going to have to tell them you are going **There**. You may have to tell them **Why**.

Depending on where your **There** is, some may laugh at you. Some may tell you:

The Stockpile of Support

- I don't see it. I don't see you **There**.
- You'll never make it **There**.
- **There** is too hard for you.
- **There** doesn't seem practical for you.
- **There** is a waste of time.
- There's more important things to worry about than **There**.
- You've never been **There** before. Why go **There** now?
- If you go **There**, what about me? I'll still be here.
- **There** is for other people, not you.
- And on, and on, and on.

However, depending on where your **There** is, some may not laugh at you. Some may tell you:

- I hope you get **There**.
- I'll help you get **There**.
- I'd like to go **There** with you.
- What can I do to help you start going **There**?
- I'll pray for you every day while you head **There**.
- I believe in you. You will get **There**. I'm confident of it.
- I can see you **There** already.
- I'll be your biggest fan the whole way **There**.
- If anyone can get **There**, it's you.
- And on, and on, and on.

The missing link is encouragement.

I sat on a manuscript for over two years. My first attempt at writing anything. It had the world's worst title (No, I'm not going to tell you), but it was words that came from my heart. I wrote it for me, but I also wrote it to encourage others.

It sat on a hard drive for two years. Then I got involved in an online mastermind group. Vegas, Ontario, Quebec, Iowa, Alabama, Vegas again. When this crowd found out I had this thing I'd been sitting on, they lit into me. I mean, they wanted to know why I'd do such a thing. Not write it. But why sit on it?

They pushed me the right way. They pushed with encouragement. They pushed with direction. They pushed with prayer. They pushed with renewed vision. They pushed until it became a real book with a real title. Then they pushed me into publishing it.

Their pushing was the encouragement I needed to get **There**.

So pick your support wisely.

- When you get discouraged, they'll be there for you.
- When you question your own motives, they'll have the positive input to get you back on track.
- When your daily habits seem more like a burden than a blessing, they'll encourage you.
- When your routines get in the way of the rest of life, they'll realize.
- When things need adjusting and tweaking, they'll help you.
- When you've hit a wall, and can't seem to go on, they will pick you up and help you over it.

The Stockpile of Support

There are three types of people who are on your side. Three types of people who want you to succeed. No one else matters outside of these three groups.

First, there are the **pushers**. They push. Pushing, in general, is not a very nice or social thing to do. I'm talking about the nice kind of push.

Parents tell their kids all the time, "Don't push your sister," or "Stop pushing your little brother." Pushing is rude, impolite, and socially unacceptable. So when we grow up, we don't push. We've learned our lesson.

I don't get in fights often. Never, honestly. But I do find myself watching a fight on TV every now and then. Not boxing, but MMA (mixed martial arts). Those guys push a lot. The pushing is two-fold for them. First, to gain an advantage over the opponent. Second, to get the opponent off balance, which I guess is gaining an advantage.

There's a reason why certain friends push you. It is not to get you off balance, but to keep you in balance. When they push, you're the one in front of them. You may be leaning too far back in your quest to get **There**.

They push because they've not been where you're heading. It's new and foreign territory for them. They may not want to go there themselves, but they know you do. Their push is an encouragement for you to go **There**.

Be thankful for the pushers in your life. Wow, that sounds a little dodgy, but you know what I mean. They want you to succeed, and when you lag behind a bit, they keep you from lagging too far back and moving forward. If they secretly wanted you to fail, they wouldn't push quite so hard.

The second type of friend in your life is the **puller**. Pullers have been there. Their **There** is similar to your **There**. They know what's ahead, and their familiarity is encouraging to you. They want you to experience getting **There**, just like they did. They pull you along, especially when the road is uphill. It usually is uphill, or it wouldn't be worth the effort.

These friends pull at different areas of your life. They pull at your heartstrings. Good friends should know what you truly love and want. They know your heart for getting **There**. They remind you of your heart commitment to this journey.

They pull at your center. Climbers wear a harness, that has loops for both legs, and a waist belt. Attached to this harness is the belay loop. It is a very important part of the harness. This is where a belay device is attached with a carabiner, or where the rope is fed through for tying into the rope. This belay loop is centrally located to your body. It is as close to your center of gravity as possible. Where the center goes, you go. Be thankful for friends so close to you that they pull at your center to keep moving forward.

The third type of friend is the **prodder**. They neither push or pull. They are not that invested in you. At least, not yet. But they are an encouragement to you. Prodding reminds me of an electric cattle motivational device. That's being nice. You stick the end on a cow, and it jolts them with a charge. Yikes. Can friends be prodders?

Prodding is meant to get you moving in the right direction. Prodders come in only two sizes.

Imagine running a race. I've done a few 5Ks, and that's about it for me. There are people along the route who prod you with words of encouragement. "You can do it." "Only 2K to go." "The finish line is around the next corner." They clap and cheer. You don't know most of them, but it doesn't matter. You appreciate the encouragement.

Now, imagine you're playing a football game. There are people there cheering for both teams. You make one little mistake, and here comes the prodding. "You suck." "You're a loser." "I can do better than that." This kind of prodding hurts. It hurts a lot. What are you going to do about this negative prodding?

Kansas City Chiefs' running back, Kareem Hunt, had never fumbled one time during his college career at the

The Stockpile of Support

University of Toledo. Drafted eighty-sixth in the third round, he started the first regular season game only because the starting running back was recovering from an injury. On his very first carry, he fumbled the ball, which was recovered by New England.

On the sidelines, Coach Andy Reid said to him, "Get ready. The first play of the next series is yours." Hunt got the ball again and ended up with two touchdowns, and 247 yards from scrimmage for the game. It was an NFL rookie record. Coach Reid is an encourager. Coach Reid knows how to prod the right way.

Can you identify people in your life who are pushers, pullers, and prodders? It's always great to know who's going to help you succeed when you tell them you're going **There**. You will find yourself looking for pullers because they've succeeded in similar efforts. You have questions, and you'd love some answers or opinions. You then look for pushers who won't talk you out of it but will be there for you along the journey to keep you from falling back. You don't look for prodders, but you will find them, or they'll find you. Prodding can go two ways. Let the negative go, and soak in the positive.

11

THE REWARD OF REPETITION

How repeatable is your process?

Whatever we plant in our subconscious minds and nourish with repetition and emotion will one day become a reality.
Earl Nightingale

Winning takes talent. To repeat it takes character.
John Wooden

Let's start this chapter off with a list of very successful failures from an article in **Business Insider**[27] back in 2015:

- Walt Disney was fired from the Kansas City Star because his editor felt he "lacked imagination and had no good ideas."

- Oprah Winfrey was publicly fired from her first television job as an anchor in Baltimore for getting "too emotionally invested in her stories."

- Steven Spielberg was rejected by the University of Southern California School of Cinematic Arts multiple times.

- R.H. Macy had a series of failed retail ventures throughout his early career.
- Soichiro Honda's unique vision got him ostracized by the Japanese business community.
- Colonel Harland David Sanders was fired from dozens of jobs before founding a fried chicken empire.
- Sir Isaac Newton's mother pulled him out of school as a boy so that he could run the family farm. He failed miserably.
- Vera Wang failed to make the 1968 US Olympic figure-skating team. Then she became an editor at *Vogue* but was passed over for the editor-in-chief position.
- Thomas Edison's teachers told him he was "too stupid to learn anything."
- When Sidney Poitier first auditioned for the American Negro Theatre, he flubbed his lines and spoke in a heavy Caribbean accent, which made the director angrily tell him to stop wasting his time and go get a job as a dishwasher.
- In one of Fred Astaire's first screen tests, an executive wrote: "Can't sing. Can't act. Slightly balding. Can dance a little."
- J.K. Rowling was a single mom living off welfare when she began writing the first *Harry Potter* novel.
- After Harrison Ford's first small movie role, an executive took him into his office and told him he'd never succeed in the movie business.
- Lucille Ball appeared in so many second-tier films at the start of her career that she became known as "The Queen of B Movies."

The Reward of Repetition

- Winston Churchill was estranged from his political party over ideological disagreements during the "wilderness years" of 1929 – 1939.
- A young Henry Ford ruined his reputation with a couple of failed automobile businesses.
- While developing his vacuum, Sir James Dyson went through 5,126 failed prototypes and his savings over fifteen years.
- Carey Mulligan was rejected from every single drama school she applied to. An auditor at Drama Center London told her to be a "children's TV show presenter" instead.
- Lady Gaga got dropped by her record label, Island Def Jam, after three months. Upon receiving the news, she "cried so hard she couldn't talk."
- Ang Lee failed Taiwan's college entrance exams—twice. Then he tried to go to acting school, but his English wasn't good enough.

Wait a second! This last element is all about repetition. Succeeding in something and doing it again.

Yes. Exactly.

All of these wildly successful people are complete failures. Failures in other people's minds. Failures earlier in life. Failures who never let that early failure define the rest of their lives. You get this list as a reminder that these supposed icons of success first learned how to fail. They failed, yet they kept going until they succeeded.

In your own effort to go **There**, you may fail. You may fail big. These people didn't stop. Failure didn't stop them. They kept moving forward every day. They chose to go there, no matter how long it took. You must see your **There** in exactly the same way. It may not be as big a creating the next Disney World (although I think that would be awesome), but your **There** is just as important, at least to you. Important to you is what's most important. It's not a competition.

Now, regarding repeating your success—creating a new **There** once your first **There** has been realized—get **There** first. Since you're on this journey, take note of how hard it is. Literally, take notes.

While serving on the staff of several local churches, I made a private file. Every time a situation didn't turn out well, I made a note of what happened, what I'd do differently the next time, then I'd file it away. I'd witness how my lead pastor (my boss) would handle a situation. Then I'd make notes of the good, or not-so-good, outcome and file it away. Ideas I tried that failed miserably? Made a note and filed it away.

Two things are at work here. First, the very act of writing down a situation, along with the outcome, made it more memorable and specific in detail. Second, I was creating a future success file.

John Wooden retired from coaching college basketball following the 1975 season with a UCLA record of 620 wins and 147 losses. Only twice during his tenure did the Bruins lose home games at Pauley Pavilion, where he coached from the 1965–66 season through the 1974–75 season. As a coach, John Wooden has won more national championships than anyone else. John Wooden repeated success. He also learned from every failure along the way.

> "Losing is only temporary and not all-encompassing.
> You must simply study it, learn from it,
> and try hard not to lose the same way again. Then you
> must have the self-control to forget about it."
> John Wooden

The Reward of Repetition

> "Success is never final. Failure is never fatal.
> It's courage that counts."
> John Wooden, again

John Wooden was known as a teacher of character as much as he was known as a successful coach. He developed a Pyramid of Success[28] which he taught to every player that came through his program, as well as at his summer camps. Nowhere in this model of fifteen attributes did it mention athletic ability. One attribute was skill, defined as "a knowledge of and the ability to properly execute the fundamentals. Be prepared. Cover every detail."

You cannot repeat unless you finish. There is no reason to keep starting new challenges and going after new goals if you don't finish the first one. There are many people who are serial starters and non-finishers.

Let's imagine for a moment that you choose something amazing to achieve in your life and ask yourself the first eight questions. That would be amazing. What would be more amazing is that you don't stop with answering the first three questions. You go on and take action with the next three questions. And you finish because you took to heart the last three questions.

You finished. You achieved. You did it. Congratulations. Now what?

Easy. Do it again! Repeat the process. Little, big, lifestyle, end-game, doesn't matter. Once a person gets a taste of success, they want to succeed again. One success can lead to another. Never settle for just one. (Like eating Lays potato chips or Oreo cookies.) Have another. I insist.

People love to be around winners. When you get **There**, people will want to be around you. Why? You've conquered something that they have not.

As I'm writing this chapter, my very first youth pastor

(from the mid-'70s) and his wife are walking the Camino de Santiago[29] in Europe. It is a hike, to say the least. The most popular route is 720 km (about 500 miles. Depending on your pace, and planning, it can take between forty to fifty days to complete.

Thurland and Lorraine Brown are in their early 60s, their collaborative **There**. This challenge fit within their purpose. They chose the Camino as a goal, then solidified their motives. They went to work through their daily habits of walking, eating right, and adjusting to whatever wrenches got in their way. Their scheme became two rears in gear, daily choosing to grit it out. (They hiked in heavy rain the first two-plus days.) And they're hiking it.

I mention this achievement because this is their second time hiking it. That's right. They did it once, and now they're doing it again. The second time is easier, but the route isn't any shorter.

You can ask the first eight questions of any challenge that you face.

1. Why are you here?

2. What do you want?

3. Why do you want it?

4. What will you do daily to get it?

5. How will your efforts work together?

6. How well will you adjust to change?

7. How desperate are you to succeed?

8. Who is going to help you get there?

With every step, every habit created, every daily push, every milestone along the way, keep a file on how you can apply the lessons learned to your next identified **There**. Call the file: "Repeatable Success."

How repeatable is your success? That depends on you. Be encouraged that you will get **There**. And when you do, you'll be better equipped for the next **There** you plan to face.

PART IV: Guaranteeing Your Arrival

If you don't learn what makes you work best and repeat it, you'll never get better.
Jon Acuff, Finish

On your next hike in the woods, stop by that babbling brook.
In the spring it may be full and fast.
In the fall it may be slow and low.
In both, there is flow.
Water doesn't come in sections. It is constant.
Flow is putting it all together and watching it succeed in your life.
Flow is essentially the fourth question.
Your flow for success is found in your daily habits.

12

WHY HABITS ARE THE HUB OF ACHIEVEMENT

People who use time wisely spend it on activities that advance their overall purpose in life.
John C. Maxwell

If you want to achieve something, anything, you'd better plan on spending some time heading in that direction.

No one should tell you what to achieve. Achievement is personal. It isn't a contest.

Let's define achievement before we look at what it takes to accomplish anything that's worth achieving.

Achievement Defined

I've backed my way into many impressive achievements over the years. Just look at part of my list. You will be impressed.

- One year while playing football, I scored 108 points in eight games. That's two and a half touchdowns per game.
- I had cancer and beat it.
- I've played the piano on stage at the Grand Ole Opry in Nashville, TN.

- I've written a #1 best-selling book.
- I've preached in front of thousands of people.
- I've backpacked in the Andes.
- I've climbed volcanos in Central America.
- I've climbed mountains in North America.
- I've four-wheeled my way along cliffs in the Rocky Mountains.
- I've played basketball with professional athletes.
- I've shared a room with the President of the United States.

The list could go on. Are you impressed? It doesn't matter. None of these are meant to impress anyone. Each one has been part of my life. Without the details, they seem much more impressive than they are. Read them again with the full story attached.

- One year while playing football, I scored 108 points in eight games. High school six-man intramural.
- I had cancer and beat it. Basal Cell Carcinoma on my lip. Outpatient surgery. Problem solved. (I don't want to diminish any cancer scare or anyone who's had cancer. However, my one statement without detail leaves too much to assumptions.)
- I've played the piano on stage at the Grand Ole Opry in Nashville, TN. I was in a leadership group that had the privilege of a private tour. While on stage, with no one but us there, I sat down at the grand piano and played a simple hymn.

- I've written a #1 best-selling book. It hit #1 in two sub-sub-sub categories on Amazon Kindle during the three-day "download it free" promotional period.

- I've preached in front of thousands of people. If you add up all the times I've preached over twenty-three years, this would be quite accurate.

- I've backpacked in the Andes. I went with a group to stay on a coffee farm for a week. My choice of luggage was a half-size backpack.

- I've climbed volcanos in Central America. Two times I signed up with a tour group to climb a volcano. The first was dormant, but quite a hike. We stayed overnight near the summit. The other was an active volcano that tourists go to almost daily. This includes people much older than me as well as five-year-olds.

- I've climbed mountains in North America. I live in Colorado. I climbed Pikes Peak in my Jeep. I made the summit of Mt. Evans in my wife's Honda Civic. I made the summit of Long's Peak on my second attempt. You'll get the details in a later chapter.

- I've four-wheeled my way along cliffs in the Rocky Mountains. Does Skyline Drive in Canon City count? I hate heights. It was nighttime. I was tricked into it. I followed the leader, and that's where he went. Intensive prayer kept me from dying.

- I've played basketball with a true professional athlete. By professional, I mean an NFL quarterback who'd been kicked out of the league for gambling. He had great potential as an athlete, but his gambling habit killed his career. I never scored that entire game.

- I've shared a room, along with a thousand other people, with the President of the United States. It was a big room. Ronald Reagan spoke at the NAE back in the '80s. I was given a ticket. I was there.

I tell you this to make a point. Achievement is relative to the individual. Comparing yourself to another can be left to the pros. It's never fair to compare.
Consider LeBron James.

"My motivation is this ghost I'm chasing," James said in an interview with Sports Illustrated. "The ghost played in Chicago."[30]

LeBron is comparing himself to the best that ever was. That's not fair to him or anyone else. Their circumstances are completely different—their teams, teammates, opponents, just about everything, including the length of their shorts.
LeBron continues . . .

"My career is totally different than Michael Jordan's. What I've gone through is totally different than what he went through. What he did was unbelievable, and I watched it unfold. I looked up to him so much. I think it's cool to put myself in position to be one of those great players, but if I can ever put myself in position to be the greatest player, that would be something extraordinary."[31]

He has this right. Totally different careers. Totally different circumstances.
The only way to quantify a comparison is statistically. Jordan has the best ever career scoring average at 30.12 ppg (points per game) in the regular season and 33.45 ppg during

Why Habits are the Hub of Achievement

the playoffs. LeBron currently averages 27.2 ppg in the regular season and 28.0 ppg during the playoffs.

Even this isn't fair. Different teams, teammates, eras, opponents, and so on. One could argue both ways about who had the better teammates with them and the better teams to compete with.

I would argue that Jordan did win three titles in a row, quit for two years to play baseball, then returned to win three more in a row. Six championships in all. Forgive me. I'm comparing circumstances.

Achievement should be relative to the individual, and not a comparison effort. When you quit comparing yourself to other people and what they've done, you are freed up to achieve more of what you truly consider an achievement.

When you start thinking about your own achievements in life, start at the end of your life. Shuffle forward to the end of your retirement years, before you kick the bucket and head into the great afterlife. Look back. What are you known for? What have you done to change someone else's life for the greater good? What did you truly achieve on purpose? What did you achieve by accident? What will others say about you when you pass?

Most people will remember you for how you treated them. People will remember the personal contact long before your statistical prowess. They will remember a conversation you had together. Or the time you went out of your way to help them on a project or prayed for them when they needed prayer.

Achievements should never wait for you to go after them. Slightly over a year ago, a school bus driver ran off the road with a busload of football players. The bus hit a bridge abutment. The only fatality was the bus driver. I do not know her achievements in life. I know nothing about her goals, aspirations, or dreams for her future. I am quite sure she didn't plan to die that day.

She never got to look back on her life and view what she had achieved. She left a lot of possibilities behind her when she passed away at such a young age. She was much younger than me.

I hate to break this to you, but you're going to die someday. It happens to everyone. For you, I hope it's not for many, many years. The problem is, you never know for sure. This is, for the most part, completely beyond our control. Don't live in fear of dying someday. Fear never living or achieving.

It's not the number of days in your life that matter. Rather, it is how you choose to live during the days you have. There are huge numbers of people who seem to have achieved so much and yet died so young. Ever wonder how they do that?

One thing is for sure. Their outlook involved today, not someday.

The "Someday Outlook" kills any achievement. If you're young, never say, "someday you'll do this or that." Just go ahead and do it.

The "Today Outlook" is the catalyst for achievement. Today is the day to start and continue something amazing.

The Hub of Achievement

I'm a very visual learner. Diagrams and pictures teach me so much more than words. When I take this idea of achievement and map it out with habits as the center of the process, this is what I come up with:

Why Habits are the Hub of Achievement

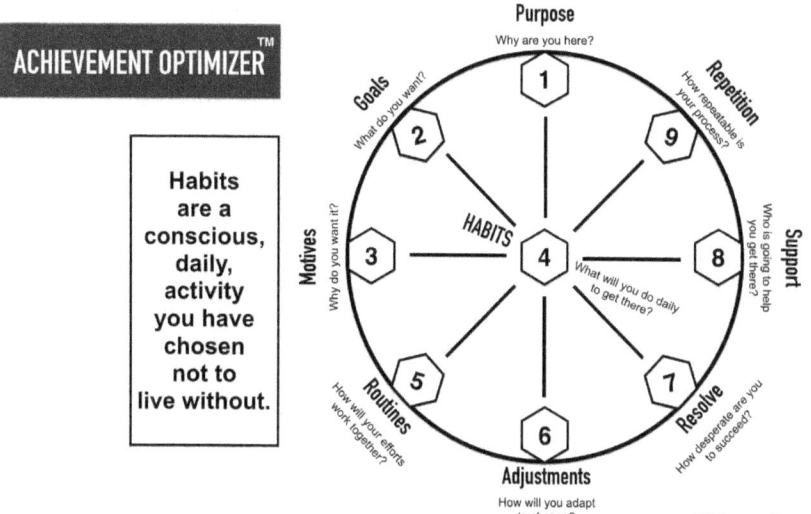

There's a connection to every question. At the center of the process are habits.

Perhaps I'm getting ahead of myself.

Question #1 deals with the overarching concept of PURPOSE.

Question #2 becomes more tangible with GOALS.

Question #3 dives deep into your MOTIVES.

Question #4 becomes the center of activity and where your achievements thrive or die.

Everything revolves around your HABITS.

Question #5 groups your habits into functional ROUTINES.

Question #6 prods you to make ADJUSTMENTS.

Question #7 deals with desperation and RESOLVE.

Question #8 brings friends into your quest for SUPPORT.

Question #9 instills in you the idea that there is a REPETITION you can apply to any future dream/goal/desire.

Questions 1-3 can be answered while sitting on the back deck in your hammock, enjoying an ice-cold lemonade or other beverage of your choice. Here you are taking your dream and scheming how you will practically accomplish it. Your dream is becoming an actual plan.

Questions 4-6 push you away from your desk and out of the chair. No more theorizing allowed. You must actively pursue your **There**. In other words, you need to get your rear in gear.

Questions 7-9 give you a backbone for achievement. They are your inner strength, outward support, and vision for future accomplishments. You will gain the grit you need to go for it.

Relationships Between the Questions

- You'll have a greater understanding of PURPOSE through Question 1. Habits need a purpose to exist. However, without regular activity in living out your purpose, you may lose sight of its very existence. Habits are the daily breath of your purpose.

- You have GOALS which you will write down in response to Question 2. Good for you. Goals are only reached by taking action. Habits are the action. Habits give goals legs.

- You will discover the MOTIVES that compel you to act to reach your goals through Question 3. Motives form our choice of habits. Goals need motives for validation. Motives also help you find ways to optimize your habits into routines.

- HABITS are addressed in Question 4 and will help determine the center of what you could do daily. They also push you to commit to the actions you will do daily.

- Question 5 helps group habits into ROUTINES— groups of daily habits working together to help you reach your goals. Habits are most effective when they're part of a routine. Like habits, routines need adjusting from time to time to remain relevant. Routines can become the synergy of habits, multiplying their effectiveness.

- Question 6 gives insight into making ADJUSTMENTS to your habits. Tweaking refocuses your habits. Adjustments also keep your routine relevant to your surrounding and schedules. Without adjustments, habits can lose sight of the overall goal.

- Question 7 shows you how RESOLVE forces you to live at 100%. Resolve powers your habits. Resolve gives confidence to any adjustment you may have to make. Resolve fuels your purpose.

- Question 8 makes you vulnerable as you seek SUPPORT. You let others, friends and associates alike, into your life. Support will help you stick to your daily habits. Those who truly support you become your accountability network.

- Question 9, regarding REPETITION, takes your habits and re-applies them to any new goal that you set your sights on achieving. Repetition makes a habit out of achievement.

Habits are a conscious, daily activity you've chosen not to live without.

Habits (Question 4) are conceived and personally defined so you can add them into your day as you stretch toward that achievement. Habits are the actions you take every single day as you step closer and closer to achieving your goal. Your success, accomplishment, achievement, goal, every reason for action, how you live out your purpose, the make-up of your routines, what and how you adjust and tweak for success, all revolve around what you do daily. What you do daily is what gets you from Here to **There**.

13

HOW YOUR DAY AFFECTS YOUR LIFE

What good have I done today?
Benjamin Franklin

Benjamin Franklin is famous for asking himself every evening, "What good have I done today?" Asking that question does two crucial things. First, it makes you take a comprehensive glance at your day and judge your effectiveness in it, allowing you to plan future days more effectively. Secondly, and most importantly, it makes you note the progress you're making towards your goals.
Xander Schultz,

The purpose of having a daily achievement goal is to use these same strategies of intense focus and clear responsibility to drive your actions on a daily basis.
Steve Jobs

As you charge forward toward wherever **There** is to you, having a daily rhythm will be the key to what keeps you on track. You will find it to be the difference between success and failure.

Without some order to your day, you become a slave to the order of someone else's day. That makes sense if you work in a job that requires you to only do what your boss wants you to do. But your job should never define you—unless you are one of those who get to define their own job. For most of us, it's just a job.

So, before you head off to do whatever your job requires of you, take control of your mornings.

Consider the following daily habits and routines that I believe are foundational to reaching any worthwhile achievement.

1. Sleep

You need enough of it. This varies from person to person. If you don't know your own sleep patterns and what you need every night, start recording when you go to bed, how long it takes you to drop off to sleep, when you wake up, how you wake up, and how long you've slept. Once you start doing this, you will have a hard time ignoring your sleep patterns.

Side note: Politics aside, I am an avid NFL football fan, and I must say I'm glad to be living in the mountain time zone. Watching a Monday night game on the east coast would totally disrupt a regular sleep habit, and would require great resolve to get up at a planned time Tuesday morning.

Almost every evening, I turn everything off at 10:00 p.m. and drop on the pillow. I'm usually asleep within ten minutes. Even though my wife stays up longer to read, I go to sleep. She has her schedule. I have mine.

Monday through Thursday I wake up at 4:30 a.m., as does my wife. Friday through Sunday, I sleep in until 5:30 a.m. This is my rhythm, not yours.

You need to find your own rhythm for sleep. Find out what works best for you, but then do it. My rule is that I can go to bed earlier if I'm tired, but my morning wake-up time rarely changes. The only exception is a late night due to a scheduled family outing or an unplanned emergency. Then, I adjust. I get back on a regular routine as soon as possible.

The key is to choose the rhythm of your own day. It should never be dictated by whatever happens to be going on that evening. Guard your sleep. Know how much you need to have a great day when you wake up.

2. Evening Routine

The best way to ensure a successful morning is to prepare for it the night before. Gone are the days of getting up, not knowing what you will wear to work. You've laid them out the night before. You no longer have a bedtime dependent on the end of a football game or late-night show. You don't make coffee in the morning, you press a button. You prepped your coffee the evening before. (I have a timer on mine, so I don't even have to press the button.) Your morning is smooth and inviting because you've planned for it the night before. A well-thought-out evening routine vastly increases your chance for success the next morning.

3. Journaling

Jim Rohn says, "If you're serious about becoming a wealthy, powerful, sophisticated, healthy, influential, cultured, and unique individual, keep a journal." These achievements may never be ones you intend to tackle. Maybe some of them are. Either way, the challenge to keep a journal is relevant. Successful people, people who achieve things in their life, make journaling a daily habit. Whether you do it in the morning or the evening is entirely up to you. Some people do both, almost like checking in for the day and checking out for the evening.

If you're not big on random writing, here are a few simple things you can do that will make a difference in your daily life.

- **Start a Gratitude Journal.** Write three things you're grateful for every day. If you journal in the evening, then it's three things you're grateful for that day. If you journal in the morning, three things you're grateful for that you may encounter that day. Try not to repeat any single item. As an option, work your way through the alphabet: Three grateful things starting with A, then B, etc.

- **Create a template to use every day.** Three wins, three things to improve, three moments that made you smile. You get the idea.

- **Keep a simple activity log.** I worked all morning, had lunch with my spouse, had a surprise visit from my boss.

- **Record the best and worst.** The best thing that happened today was ____. The worst thing that happened today was ____. What did I learn from both?

I mentioned earlier that I create an entry every day in a digital filing system called Evernote.[32] A benefit of using this app is I can take a selfie (yes, a selfie) and add it to the file. I do this so in forty years when I'm dead and gone, my daughter will have way too many pictures of her dad. Not a bad thing.

4. Exercise

I hate it. Not a fan. I'm not lazy, but I'm not overly motivated to move my body on a regular basis. Nevertheless, I walk the dog for at least thirty minutes every morning, and I do a 7-Minute-Workout app on my phone (which takes seven minutes and fifty seconds). When the weather turns cold, as it seems to do annually here in Colorado, I will start jogging on the treadmill. Yes, we own a treadmill. Yes, it gets used. And, yes, it's used to dry clothes from time to time. Not gonna lie.

There is a consensus among a majority of lifestyle gurus who write articles. It seems that regular exercise is an absolute necessity to develop your best daily habits, live a long life, be happier, overcome depression, be healthy, and so on.

Google "best daily habits" and see what pops up. Here's what popped up for me when I did it:

- 34 Morning Daily Routine Habits ...
- 203 Good Daily Habits ...
- 25 Best Habits ...
- 9 Daily Habits ...
- 24 Daily Habits ...
- 19 Simple Daily Habits ...
- 35 Business Leaders Share Their Daily Habits ...
- 12 Daily Habits You Should Adopt ...

These are the first eight of about 7,310,000 entries. Every article mentions exercise. Not these first eight, in case you're wondering. Since what you're reading right now is a list of suggested daily habits, I concur with my colleagues wholeheartedly. If you're not convinced by me and over seven million others, ask your doctor.

5. Devotion/Prayer

As a Christian, this is an essential part of my own personal spiritual growth. I practice a self-created 30-Minute-Morning for this one area alone. I begin with one minute of deep breathing, listen to one worship song via headphones, read a portion of Scripture, and write down personal thoughts. I spend time in prayer and write in my journal on my iPad, which I mentioned above. I have a prayer journal, a Moleskin, in which I keep handwritten prayers and lists.

You can get a copy of my 30 Minute Morning routine checklist at https://billmcconnell.me/30-minute-ebook/

6. Meditation

Experimenting with the idea of meditation back in January 2017, I committed forty days to using a guided meditation app called Headspace.[33] I enjoyed it much more than I thought I would, and I was not recruited to join any eastern religions while doing so (a misconception some people have). Ten minutes every morning to focus on breathing deeply, concentrating on nothing, and being calm. I was amazed at the results in my own life. I have continued the practice without using the app, but am reconsidering that decision to maintain the focus. The narrator sounds Australian and the accent, believe it or not, is not a distraction.

7. Reading

My goal this year (2017) is to read thirty books. I do this every morning, and add some additional reading time right after lunch. I keep a running list of books I plan to read and check off those I've finished. Compiling a list ahead of time means, when I'm done with one, I don't sit around and wonder what to read next. The list of thirty was only about half a list at the beginning of the year because new books and recommendations will catch my attention. I have no fear of not filling out and completing my list and reading my target amount.

8. Morning Mantra

I saved this one for last because I'm going to get a little more in-depth with it. Hope you don't mind. (You won't.)

It is a challenge to create a morning mantra for yourself. Yes, a morning mantra. Hang with me on this. You won't regret it.

What's a Mantra? Merriam-Webster says this;

: a sound, word, or phrase that is repeated by someone who is praying or meditating

   : a word or phrase that is repeated often or that expresses someone's basic beliefs

I challenge you to create a morning mantra to recite every morning before you do anything else. If you're married, this may freak out your spouse a bit. Oh well.

Now I know the idea of a morning mantra may bring up the idea of Hindu practice, yoga, or other eastern religions. That's not where I'm going. Where I am going is to get you in the habit of saying something to yourself every morning before anything else. It is the practice of daily affirmation.

You won't be alone in this effort. The concept has been around for centuries. Hal Elrod, the author of *The Miracle Morning*, has this to say about the concept of morning affirmations.

> Your affirmations are either working for you or against you, depending on how you use them. If you don't consciously design and choose your affirmations, you are susceptible to repeating and reliving the fears, insecurities, and limitations of your past. However, when you actively design and write out your affirmations to be in alignment with what you want to accomplish and who you need to be to accomplish it—and commit to repeating them daily (ideally out loud)—they immediately make an impression on your subconscious mind. Your affirmations go to work to transform the way you think and feel so you can overcome your limiting beliefs and behaviors and replace them with those you need to succeed.
>
>   Hal Elrod, *The Miracle Morning*[34]

Talking to yourself may seem weird at first. That's how I felt when I first started doing it. I come from a rather negative upbringing. My father wasn't very supportive of anything I wanted to do. There were always comments like: "You'll never be able to do that." "It's too hard for you." "That's something you need to be afraid of." He was speaking his own fears over my life, and I didn't know any better than to let him. As a result, I've spent much of my adult years hearing Dad's voice in the back of my mind.

Once I realized I didn't have to listen to that voice anymore, I started looking for other voices to listen to. Positive voices. Affirming voices.

Not everyone grows up with this negative voice in their head. Mine was implanted over the first twenty years of my life. That was a lot of years. It continues to hang around to this very day. I found that even when I began talking positively to myself, I didn't believe it. I kept doing it anyway. I wanted to believe it. I do believe it. After all, no one should be controlled by their past.

One of the best ways to reach your own goals in life is to start talking yourself into believing those achievements can take place in you.

My challenge to you is to craft your own morning affirmation. Make it positive, personal, and proactive.

One statement to kick off your day. Here are a few suggestions:

- Today, I am thankful for _____. (Gratitude)

- Today, I will accomplish _____. (Goal)

- Today, I will take one step closer to _____. (Goal)

- My intention for today is _____. (Attitude)

- What would you have me do today, Lord? (Prayer)
- I will do whatever has to be done to _____. (Productivity)
- I will focus on the important, not the urgent. (Stephen Covey)
- I will work to answer the nine Questions of Achievement.

If you think you need more suggestions, go to Pinterest and search "morning mantra." The options are endless and vary widely, depending on the belief systems of the originators. Be selective according to your own circumstances.

When beginning a new habit like this one, you will most likely forget to do it tomorrow morning. Eventually, you will remember, and you will do it. It'll seem awkward, but don't let that stop you. Say it word for word. Say it like you mean it. Say it because you mean it.

I always follow a few simple rules when writing my mantra, which I review and change every quarter.

Rule #1: Use first person.
"I will _____."
"I can _____."
"Today I will _____."

Rule #2: Keep sentences short. Better three short sentences than one long one. Easier to remember, and easier to scream and scare your spouse. Hehe.

Rule #3: Write it down, and make it the first thing you grab when you get out of bed. For me, it's my glasses, phone, iPad, and planner. My affirmations are in my planner. Yeah, I'm that guy. You should be, too.

Rule #4: Adjust when necessary. You're not stuck in one little chant for the rest of your life. I review and change mine every quarter to be in alignment with my quarterly goals.

Your morning mantra should push you forward for the day. Your first repeatable daily habit should send you in the direction of your purpose and goals.

Try this simple template. Use part of it or all of it.

I will _____ (Purpose & Goal)

I will because _____ (Motive)

Today I will _____ (Habits)

Today I will work my ROUTINES regardless.

Today I will ADJUST so life won't interrupt my progress.

I consider these my absolute essentials for any given day. I adjust for family and vacation, as anyone would.

You get to decide on your own morning mantra. Write it down. Hone the wording. Make it yours.

There's a good reason for telling you some of the main habits of my day, particularly my morning. I rely on them. A lot. They propel me into each day with purpose and resolve. There are times when I don't have achievement goals, but I always have lifestyle goals and purpose. My purpose is solidified every morning with my routines and habits. I don't die if I miss a day or two. I've resolved never to miss any more than two days at a time. I'm aiming for just one miss, and that will come soon as family schedules adjust.

Your days, and what you put in them, are your choice alone. I've given you a great start. Resolve means embracing new experiences in life. When you choose to order your life, you take control of your life. You control the day.

WARNING: You will fail in implementing order into your life. So what. Keep at it. The world around you will conspire to throw you off your game. Don't let it. You will never get **There** with random days and partial focus. When you instill daily habits into your life as listed above, you can drop **There** into every one of them.

1. Sleep: **There** is the last thing you say to yourself before nodding off to la-la-land.

2. Evening Routine: **There** is written on a piece of paper sitting on your night table.

3. Journaling: **There** is mentioned in every entry in one way or another.

4. Exercise: **There** is your vision as you get in shape, seeing yourself **There** and healthy.

5. Devotion: **There** is what you pray about as part of your time with God.

6. Meditation: **There** is a single focus point visualized for a period of time.

7. Reading: **There** is a topic of your reading habit. Pick books that point **There**.

8. Morning Mantra: **There** is a main part of your morning mantra. State it. Restate it.

Sounds a little obsessive, doesn't it? Good. You have permission to be obsessed with something you want to achieve. The less obsessed you are, the farther away **There** is.

14
THE ACHIEVEMENT OPTIMIZER™ VISUALIZED

If a picture is worth a thousand words, what's a good graphic worth?
Bill McConnell, Author

There are two types of achievement goals. These are goals attached to your purpose and driven by your motives.

First, there are **lifestyle goals**. These are goals that you want to reach and stay at. Goals like quitting smoking or reaching a target weight and maintaining it.

Then, there are **achievement goals**. These are goals like climbing that mountain, getting that promotion, running that 5K, earning that degree.

Once you choose to go **There** and get **There**, you realize it is a repeatable formula. Pick a new **There**. Work the process again and again.

Re-establish or reaffirm your Why, your purpose in life.
Purpose: Why are you here?

Define your next achievement.
The Goal: What do you want?

**Reason your way through every
pro and con for you going there.**
Motives: Why do you want it?

[Here is the line in the sand. Between planning **There** to heading **There**.]

**Identify and commit to only the best daily habits
for the best results.**
*Habits: What will you do daily to get **There**?*

**Create a daily rhythm so your
habits will become synergistic.**
Routine: How will your efforts work together?

Expect wrinkles, wrenches, and alternate routes.
Adjustment: How will you adapt to change?

[This is where grit kicks in and gets you **There**]

100% is easy. 99% is hard.
Resolve: How desperate are you to succeed?

No one succeeds alone. There's always a helping hand.
*Support: Who is going to help you get **There**?*

Once is luck. Repeated success shows true character.
Repetition: How repeatable is your success?

This is what I look at every day. I have it printed and sitting on my desk beside my monitor.

It is the AchievementOptimizer:

The Achievement Optimizer™ Visualized

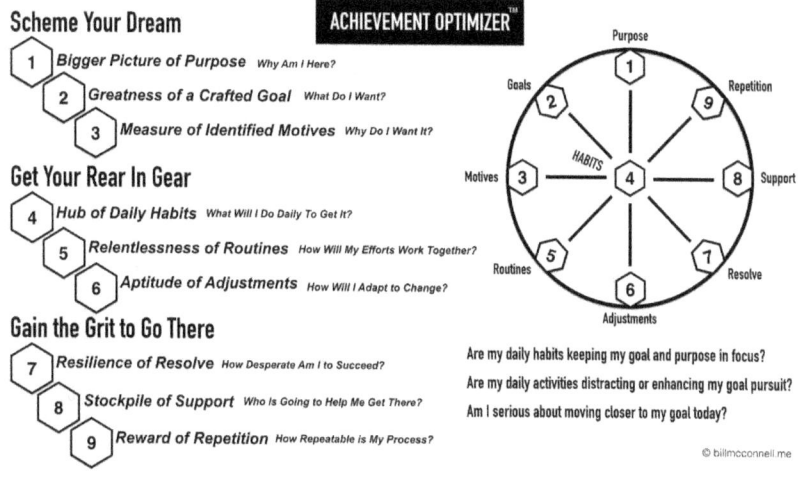

You can get your one-page graphic of the AchievementOptimizer™ at DoingStuffDaily.com/Optimize

What follows are the links and relationships of the AchievementOptimizer™. First, the planning phase:

Q1: Why are you here? PURPOSE

- Goals should flow from a great Purpose.
- Habits need Purpose for existence.
- Purpose fuels Resolve.

Q2: What do you want? GOALS

- Goals need a greater Purpose than the Goal itself.
- Goals need Motives for validation.
- Habits move you towards your Goals.

Q3: Why do you want it? MOTIVES

- Motives validate your Goal.
- Motives are what ultimately form your Habits.
- Motives help optimize your Routines.

Q4: What would you do daily to get it? HABITS

- Habits are formed from your Motives.
- Habits are the means to achieve your Goals.
- Habits derive from a strong life Purpose.

Q5: How will your efforts work together? ROUTINES

- Motives optimize Routines.
- Routines increase the effectiveness of each Habit.
- Routines need to be Adjusted to remain relevant.

Q6: How will you adapt to change? ADJUSTMENT

- Adjustments refocus your Habits.
- Adjustments keep your Routines relevant.
- Resolve keeps you Adjusting so you don't lose ground.

Q7: How desperate are you to succeed? RESOLVE

- Your Purpose fuels your Resolve.
- Resolve powers your Habits.
- Resolve keeps you Adjusting so you can move forward.

Q8: Who is going to help you get there? SUPPORT

- Your Support reinforces your Resolve.
- Your Support empowers your Habits.
- Support is a reflection of your Purpose in others.

Q9: How repeatable is your success? REPETITION

- Your Repetition of success becomes a Habit.
- Your Repetition reinforces your daily Habits.
- Repetition is the greatest motivation needed to continue.

The Idea of FLOW

How repeatable is your success? I'll answer this one for you. It is very repeatable. It is also very adaptable.

On your next hike in the woods, stop by that babbling brook. In the spring, it may be full and fast. In the fall, it may be slow and low. In both, there is flow. Water doesn't come in sections. It is constant. Flow is putting it all together and watching it succeed in our lives.

Flow is essentially the fourth question and the definition of habits. Your flow for success is found in your daily habits.

I'm serious when I ask this: Does the world need another acronym? I guess the answer is subjective. Nevertheless, here is an acronym for **FLOW**.

F – Focus: Dialing in on your goals daily, and working toward them, requires focus. Forgive me, but here's the acronym within an acronym for the word **"focus"** that I absolutely love: Follow One Course Until Complete. I guess there's always room for one more acronym.

L – Lifestyle: Having daily habits is a lifestyle. All of us have subconscious habits we do daily so that we don't have to think about them. Do you remember the definition I gave you for habits? *Habits are a conscious, daily activity you've chosen not to live without.* Choose your habits and live on purpose. Make achievement a lifestyle. When you do, you will find repeatable success in setting and achieving goals in your life.

O – Optimize: Make the most effective use of any given situation and system. Make the best use of these questions. Use them to pursue your purpose, go after your goals, mastermind your motives, hone your habits, craft your course of action, rely on your routines, accept having to adjust, and resolve to never rest until you get **There**.

W – Win: Some may say I failed on my first attempt to climb Long's Peak. Maybe. I say it prepared me to succeed the second time. You can view failure one of two ways: Either you blew it and you're a loser, or you prepare to win. You're either winning, or you're preparing to win. Your only competition is you. Don't forget that.

So, where are you headed? Where is **There**?

15
THERE YOU GO AGAIN

Out of the night that covers me,
Black as the pit from pole to pole,
I thank whatever gods may be
For my unconquerable soul.

In the fell clutch of circumstance
I have not winced nor cried aloud.
Under the bludgeonings of chance
My head is bloody, but unbowed.

Beyond this place of wrath and tears
Looms but the Horror of the shade,
And yet the menace of the years
Finds and shall find me unafraid.

It matters not how strait the gate,
How charged with punishments the scroll,
I am the master of my fate,
I am the captain of my soul.

Invictus, William Ernest Henley

It is said that Nelson Mandela would repeat this poem during his low periods, while imprisoned for twenty-seven years in South Africa. He fought for equality and freedom from slavery. His purpose was clear, and his goal was to survive so his purpose could live.

> *There is no easy walk to freedom anywhere, and many of us will have to walk through the valley of the shadow of death again and again before we reach the mountaintop of our desires.*
> Nelson Mandela

I pray neither you nor I will find ourselves in prison for any reason. If anyone had a reason to give up, it would be Nelson Mandela. Our walk from Here to **There** may not be through the valley of the shadow of death, but then again, maybe it will be. Please keep in mind, your **There** doesn't have to be of the same magnitude as Mandela's. It may seem as big at times, but only to you. Simply keep going. Every day will draw you closer.

I will probably never go to the top of Vulcan Acatenango ever again. Good thing. That hike was a killer. But sometime in the next year or two, I will do the hike from Bear Lake to Grand Lake. Fifteen plus miles in Rocky Mountain National Park. It's another **There** for me to chase after.

I also plan to write a book every year. It's an annual goal of mine. This is my second. I need to rewrite my first one. It needs a 2.0 update. I already know the topic and outline of my third book. Right about now, my good friend is cringing at the thought of proofreading one of my books every single year. Another **There**.

I'm already answering the ninth question and repeating my personal success with new achievements.

My purpose is set. I'm here to help others. I'm here to help you. My goals will shift and change over time and so will yours. With every new **There**, reasons and motives will help point the way.

As my days are filled with habits and routines, each one keeps me on track to move closer to another goal, another **There**. It's the daily commitment to control the little things in life that allow me to chip away at the big ones I've chosen to master. Get your day under control, and getting **There** will be a smoother ride.

Somewhere in the future, there will be wrinkles. I'm not a doomsday kind of guy, but let's face it, life is never a bed of roses. Unforeseen thorns await. Neither is it a yellow brick road to success. I have to be honest. Those flying monkeys still haunt me to this day. Just adjust. It will be okay.

Flying monkeys, or flying wrenches, should never deter you. Duck and keep going. You've already decided to get **There** regardless. Your friends want you to as well. Some will go along for the ride.

I have one last thing to ask of you:
What's next for you and how are you going to conquer it?

ACKNOWLEDGMENTS

When inspiration hits, you need to act. It's as simple as that. My wife is the one who pushes and prods me forward in the best possible way. This book would never be in your hands without her support and encouragement. She is a Family Nurse Practitioner who loves her patients one at a time.

My globe-trotting missionary daughter loves to outdo her dad, and I'm okay with that. This one time, I wouldn't let her top off a volcano without it being on my list of achievements done. Well, you know the rest of the story. You did read the book, didn't you?

My fellow adventurer, Tim Johnston, is more than a good friend. He is a stellar proofreader and strong supporter of my personal growth. He is chapter 10 to me. Did I mention he's an engineer in the oil and gas industry with his own consulting company? He's multitalented.

The support of Author Academy Elite (AAE), the super-supportive Igniting Souls Tribe, and leader/publisher Kary Oberbrunner are unmatched. Without the mass of support and knowledge, this book would be lost on a hard drive or stuffed in the dusty basement corners of Amazon.com self-published purgatory. See chapter 10 once again.

ENDNOTES

1. Martinale, Kenneth, Nolan Ryan, Tom House and Steroids, August 11, 2014 http://radicalbaseball.blogspot.com/2014/08/nolan-ryan-tom-house-and-steroids.html
2. Robbins, Danny, The Day After Is Routine : Baseball: Nolan Ryan, taking his seventh no-hitter in stride, goes back to work, May 3, 1991 http://articles.latimes.com/1991-05-03/sports/sp-1229_1_nolan-ryan
3. Charles Duhigg, The Power of Habit, Why We Do What We Do in Life and Business (United States of America: Random House 2012), chap. 1, Kindle.
4. "Sacred Pact Dialogue" The Karate Kid. Amazon Prime Video. Directed by John G. Avildsen. 1984. Columbia Pictures.
5. Thomas Selk and Tom Bartow, with Matthew Rudy, Organize Tomorrow Today: 8 Ways to Retrain Your Mind to Optimize Performance at Work and in Life (United States of America: Da Capo Press, 2015), chap. 1, Kindle.
6. How to Bullet Journal, May 21, 2015 https://www.youtube.com/watch?v=fm15cmYU0IM
7. How to Get a Grip on Your Higher Purpose, Episode 26: Interview with Kevin Monroe, Coffee For Your Soul Podcast, October 3, 2017. https://billmcconnell.me/purpose-interview-kevin-monroe/
8. Hyatt, Michael, 5 Days to Your Best Year Ever, 2013. https://bestyearever.me/ 2013. NOTE: This was his first

year offering this online course. Link is to his current edition.
9. Burchard, Brendan, How NOT to Set Goals (Why S.M.A.R.T. goals are lame) YouTube, July 12, 2014 https://www.youtube.com/watch?v=54aFTZ9POw4.
10. Robbins, Mel, Mel Robbins on Why Motivation is Garbage – Impact Theory. January 31, 2017 https://www.youtube.com/watch?v=LCHPSo79rB4
11. "Cab Dialogue" Collateral. Amazon Prime Video. Directed by Michael Mann. 2004. Paramount Studio
12. Clear, James. The 3 R's of Habit Change: How to Start New Habits That Actually Stick. https://jamesclear.com/three-steps-habit-change
13. Clear, James, Forget About Setting Goals. Focus On This Instead. https://jamesclear.com/goals-systems?__vid=c3eef000547a0132ca9c22000b2a88d7
14. Clear, The 3 R's of Habit Change.
15. Tynan, Superhuman by Habit: A Guide to Becoming the Best Possible Version of Yourself, One Tiny Habit at a Time. Self-published on Amazon.com, chap. 3 Kindle.
16. Tynan, Superhuman By Habit.
17. Trapani, Gina. Jerry Seinfeld's Productivity Secret. https://lifehacker.com/281626/jerry-seinfelds-productivity-secret
18. Clear, James. How to Stop Procrastinating On Your Goals By Using The "Seinfeld Strategy." https://jamesclear.com/stop-procrastinating-seinfeld-strategy
19. Sara, Do This One Thing Every Day to Guarantee Success and Do Work You Love. http://unsettle.org/routine/
20. Martinale, Kenneth, Nolan Ryan, Tom House and Steroids, August 11, 2014 http://radicalbaseball.blogspot.com/2014/08/nolan-ryan-tom-house-and-steroids.html

21. "Closing Monologue." The Martian. Amazon Prime Video. Directed by Ridley. 2015. 20th Century Fox.
22. Thomas Selk, Ten Minute Toughness: The Mental-Training Program for Winning Before the Game Begins (New York: McGraw Hill, 2009)
23. Nicki Jhabvala, Few survive the hell Von Miller endured this offseason. The Man is on a mission. The Denver Post, July 29, 2017 http://www.denverpost.com/2017/07/29/von-miller-on-a-mission-broncos/
24. Pyambu Tuul, http://www.dnaindia.com/sports/report-olympics-moments-marathon-man-tuul-was-blind-for-20-years-1708930
25. 10 Unbelievable Summer Olympic Moments, August 30, 2016, https://www.youtube.com/watch?v=69qbRtoH7rw.
26. Olympics Inspiration: Finish the Race, Not Just Start It!, March 29, 2012, YouTube, https://www.youtube.com/watch?v=k6oW9uYtJnA
27. Sugar, Rachel, Richard Feloni and Ashley Lutz, 29 Famous People Who Failed Before They Succeeded. Business July 9, 2015. Insider http://www.businessinsider.com/successful-people-who-failed-at-first-2015-7/
28. Pyramid of Success. http://www.coachwooden.com/pyramid-of-success
29. Camino de Santiago: More Than a Walk. Episode 35: Interview with Thurland and Lorraine Brown, Coffee For Your Soul Podcast, December 5, 2017. https://billmcconnell.me/camino/
30. Jenkins, Lee, LeBron James Chases the Ghost From Chicago and Basketball Immoertality. Sports Illustrated, August 2, 2016. https://www.si.com/nba/2016/08/02/lebron-james-michael-jordan-ghost-cleveland-cavaliers-championship
31. Lee, Sports Illustrated.
32. Evernote is productivity app for use across multiple devices. https://evernote.com

33. Headspace is a medication app for your smartphone. https://www.headspace.com
34. Hal Elrod, The Miracle Morning: The Not-So-Obvious Secret Guaranteed to Transform Your Life before 8am. Hal Elrod International, 2017. chap. 6 Kindle

ABOUT THE AUTHOR

What? You don't know enough about me already. C'mon.

Bill McConnell is a 23-year veteran of local church ministry. He's earned a Masters in Church Leadership and is a Certified Project Manager. He loves it when a plan comes together. He currently blogs at billmcconnell.me and promotes the nine questions of this book at doingstuffdaily.com. He has a faith-based podcast he cohosts with Jamey French down there in Las Vegas. Married for at least 37 years and counting to the most loving and supportive wife in the world, Lisa, a Nurse Practitioner with a heart and gift for serving the substance abuse and mental health population. Yup, only one daughter, home from the mission field, living in our basement with her rabbit (It's not as crazy as it sounds) and working with children in a bilingual setting.

Want to know more? Just ask.

Email: bill@billmcconnell.me and mention how you got hold of my email. It's supposed to be a secret. Sort of. Not anymore, I guess.

Twitter: @DoingStuffDaily
Facebook.com/doing-stuff-daily
Websites: BillMcConnell.me and DoingStuffDaily.com
Find Bill's Podcast on iTunes: Doing Stuff Daily

GET YOUR COPY OF
THE ACHIEVEMENT OPTIMIZER

A visual reminder to help you work through the 9 questions of continued achievement

- PDF graphic can be used as wallpaper on your monitor.
- It is print quality so you can put it wherever you wish

ACCESS YOUR
FREE GRAPHIC AT
DoingStuffDaily.com/Optimize

WHEN THERE'S A HILL TO CLIMB DON'T THINK THAT WAITING WILL MAKE IT ANY SMALLER.

unknown

CONQUER WHAT'S NEXT
ONLINE COURSE

In our minds, hills turn into mountains the longer we wait. Your dream is a hill that's waited long enough.

Discover a proven path to planning hyour dream and embark on a transformational journey of daily habits that will keep you on track to conquer whatever's next in your life.

FIND OUT MORE AT
DoingStuffDaily.com/Conquer

Bring Bill into your organization

As a speaker for over 20 years, you will not be disappointed with Bill at your next meeting / retreat / conference.

- Finghting Internal Apathy
- The 9 Questions That Will Change Your Life
- Execution and Resolve
- Why Habit Are the Key to Success
- You Morning is the Key to Conquering

PRESS KIT
& CONTACT INFORMATION
AVAILABLE AT

DoingStuffDaily.com/Speaker

DOING STUFF DAILY

Daily Habits That Shape Your Life

Get practical insights and fresh ideas every week by tuning in each week.

Dive deeper into the nine questions that make up the Achievement Optimizer process.

Find the podcast AND show notes at DoingStuffDaily.com/Podcast

or... search for us on iTunes

www.ingramcontent.com/pod-product-compliance
Lightning Source LLC
LaVergne TN
LVHW011817060526
838200LV00053B/3818